IMAGINING EINSTEIN

Essays on M-Theory, World Peace &
The Science of Compassion

*Tom
thank you so much for becoming
The change!*

By Barbara With

Mad Island Communications LLC
La Pointe, WI

IMAGINING EINSTEIN
ESSAYS ON M-THEORY, WORLD PEACE &
THE SCIENCE OF COMPASSION.
© 2007 Barbara With
ISBN 978-0-9677458-7-9
Library of Congress Control Number: 2007921709

For information, address
Mad Island Communications LLC
P.O. Box 153
La Pointe, WI 54850

www.barbarawith.com

ACKNOWLEDGMENTS

A generous thanks goes to the La Pointe Center for funding this project; to Teresa McMillian and Lily Phelps, for being my best friends and the guinea pigs in this unearthly and miraculous study; to Susan Sabre for wading through this material word for word with me; to Keren and Batya at IFP Enterprises for helping get this book into the world; to Sandy Adler for attention to detail and editing; to JJ Nelson for giving me a soft place to fall; to everyone at Lake Superior Interfaith Community Church for being my congregation; to Robert Hartzell for bringing me to this island in the first place; to Dave Zielinski for his support of all my creative efforts; and to Albert Einstein, my inspiration, may he once again revolutionize the way we see the world.

This book is dedicated to my friends and neighbors of Madeline Island. Thank you for allowing me to birth this revolution amongst you. Sharing this hallowed ground means we are all keepers of the truth of unity. It is an honor to be on this island with you.

God bless us all.

TABLE OF CONTENTS

INTRODUCTION

In 1905, Albert Einstein brought the world the theory of relativity, which forever changed the way we understand the universe. Not just a brilliant scientist, Einstein was also a tireless activist for world peace. His legacy lives on years after his passing: 2005 was dedicated "The Year of Physics" by the United Nations as a tribute to the 100-year anniversary of his "miracle year" that included $E=MC^2$; The Albert Einstein Institute, founded in 1983, is dedicated to advancing the study and use of strategic nonviolent action in conflicts throughout the world.

One of the great challenges that Einstein faced in both the scientific and global arenas was finding a unified field theory, which, to this day, has not completely been accomplished. The basic problem is that, in the microcosm, physics appear to react and respond differently than in the macrocosm. So, too, with world peace: Einstein could find small communities that supported peace in the "microcosm" of their world, but he could not understand how to bring unity to the "macrocosm" of many nations with varied beliefs and world views.

One hundred years after Einstein's discovery of relativity, the planet Earth has never been more armed and dangerous. With the mass proliferation of nuclear weapons, we are literally rigged for explosion like a suicide bomber. One wrong move on the part of a government or independent terrorist group could literally destroy life as we know it.

Einstein saw this possibility, and before his death in 1955 penned a paper with his friend and colleague Bertrand Russell called the Russell-Einstein Manifesto. This paper

was presented in London three months after his death and
signed by prominent members of the scientific community.
It foretold of possibilities of a violent and dangerous world
much like the one we live in today. Einstein and Russell
issued a sobering warning and included the following
resolution:

> We invite this Congress, and through it the
> scientists of the world and the general public, to
> subscribe to the following resolution: In view of the
> fact that in any future world war, nuclear weapons
> will certainly be employed, and that such weapons
> threaten the continued existence of mankind,
> we urge the governments of the world to realize,
> and to acknowledge publicly, that their purpose
> cannot be furthered by a world war, and we urge
> them, consequently, to find peaceful means for the
> settlement of all matters of dispute between them.

"Imagining Einstein" is a series of essays based on a
premise of "what ifs": What if there really is an Afterlife,
and what if, in that Afterlife, Einstein discovered the
answers to the questions that so plagued him in life? What
if we could somehow communicate with him? What would
he say? What could he tell us to advance science, but more
importantly, bring peace to our world before it's too late?

Einstein once said that imagination is more important
than knowledge. This book is the product of my imagination
as well as extensive research into the mysterious world of
quantum physics and string theory. I suppose we should
call it science fiction. I closed my eyes and imagined I
was talking to Einstein. I saw him sitting in front of me,

looking much like he did in 1904, before his miracle year: young, wide eyed, without pretense, just an ordinary man imagining extraordinary things. From his unique position reporting directly from the space between the molecules, Einstein's speculations about the nature of Afterlife, the manifestation of matter, a unified field theory, and world peace present a quantum view of consciousness from 10^{-100} and provide answers on how to attain global peace that begins within each individual.

However you classify this, it is my hope that this work can create an awareness and dialogue around both science and peace, and inspire individuals to look at their lives in a new way. Let "Imagining Einstein" spark your own imagination to ponder these issues. Allow it inspire you to find new solutions to old problems by looking deeply into your own life. Use it to expand your awareness to include the infinite possibilities that exist that you might not be able to see just yet.

I believe that we as a species will find a path to peace, and I believe that path starts within each individual. If we wish to see our beautiful Earth live on, we must find creative solutions that will ensure a place for our children's children to live in the truth of unity. We cannot find these solutions from the same mind set as we created the problems. Our minds must expand to survive. If this book can spark even a glimmer of movement towards that expansion within you, then its purpose will be served.

Barbara With
Madeline Island, Wisconsin, 2007

THE NATURE OF AFTERLIFE

It is not unusual for those who have passed into Afterlife to communicate with those who remain focused on the physical world. This isn't hard to understand if you consider that, at this very moment, a part of your energy, even as you're experiencing physical life, exists in Afterlife and is subject to the laws of Afterlife, as I am now. But because your physical existence is dependent on being focused so intently on physical reality, you convince yourself that this other part of you doesn't exist, merely because you are not conscious of it yet.

Those of us "on the other side" experience things quite differently. We see ourselves as just like you, beings of energy, but we have merely lost our focus on ordinary matter. This does not mean that the world of matter does not exist for us. We just experience it in a different way: your hard reality is like a dream to us, and your dreams and imagination are the interface where we meet and work.

Consider this: only about 5% of the Universe is made up of what is called "ordinary matter." That is the stuff of the hard objects of your body, the table, the planets, the stars, the galaxies, etc. That leaves approximately 95% of the Universe unaccounted for. In my day we called it "ether." Today's scientists call it "dark matter" and "dark energy." Dark matter has no light within it; it can only be detected by its gravitational waves. This is the matter of Afterlife and the energy of consciousness.

THE MATHEMATICS OF KARMA

Your physical body is indeed your temple, where during the course of a lifetime knowledge of your empirical experiences compiles in your cells as photons of information. These photons are the quantum of the electromagnetic energy of your consciousness. They contain all the "if P then Qs" of what took place in your life. Every decision that you make during the course of your lifetime has a math. When you decide to turn right instead of left, say yes instead of no, sit still instead of move forward, you create a living mathematics, a series of formulas that then determines the direction of your life. This math is embedded into a unit of consciousness, called a "compilation" and stored in the photons that become the sum of this knowledge and the basis of your identify.

A compilation of consciousness has zero mass and an infinite lifetime. At 10^{-100} a compilation emits gravitational waves that pulse through dark energy and incite dark matter to cluster. How your consciousness experiences itself, both in life and after the death of the physical body, is determined by the math of these gravitational waves.

The gravity of your consciousness is indeed a compilation. Its math consists of a combination of the math of Earth's gravitational waves, the math you bring with you into physical life, the empirical experience you compile while creating a physical body, and what consciousness is focused on at the point when the physical body dies. What you are focused on and the memories and emotions of your physical life become like a negative of a photograph with a map of your identity. This map is imprinted on the gravitational waves of your consciousness and determines how the dark matter will cluster once your physical body dies. Therefore, the quality of the life you live will determine the condition of your death.

Think of it this way: Earth is constantly emitting gravitational waves from its core. These waves are the product of the warping of spacetime in the center of the Earth as the core spins hotter and faster than the rest of the planet. The iron in the core provides a magnetic path for the electricity produced by the gravitation waves coiling around the core. This electromagnetic energy becomes the primal element in the manifestation of matter on the planet.

You, the singular compilation of consciousness, are constructed in the same fashion. Your compilation emits gravitational waves from your core. Each compilation on the wave has the same unique math. Operating like the Earth, your gravity coils around the core of your compilation, producing magnetic waves, and this electromagnetic energy becomes the foundation of the ordinary matter you experience, first and foremost of which is your own physical body.

The idea of these photons compiling as consciousness is equivalent to the concept of the soul. Your soul is allegedly your animating and vital principle credited with faculties of thought, emotion and action conceived in the form of an immaterial entity distinguished from but temporarily coexistent with the body. This is exactly how consciousness behaves in a compilation.

The information contained within these photons is the animating force of your physical body, without which your body would merely be a mass of tissues, bones and water. When your body dies, these photons return to pure energy and transfer the knowledge of that lifetime directly into the gravity of your consciousness. Retaining the information, consciousness pulses through the dark energy, causing the dark matter to cluster in ways specific to that gravity. In this way, the soul lives on after the death of the physical body.

THE GRAVITY OF YOUR CHOICES

The system in which consciousness creates matter is both a determinant and free-will system. The math of your gravity creates something of a destiny that your consciousness is locked into. Yet free will gives you the power over your own domain, your thoughts, your feelings, your perceptions, your actions, and therefore the power to re-determine the frequency of your gravity that can then change your destiny. How you direct your free will in life will determine the destiny of your Afterlife.

On your deathbed life doesn't actually "flash before your eyes." The transfer of knowledge into energy is the sum and consequences of all decisions made in life. This is truly the moment of judgment, but not as if some hand reaches out and deems you on your way to heaven or hell. Instead, as the knowledge in your body changes into pure energy, something of a cause and effect takes place. You gain the energy compiled by all the knowledge acquired from your every action and subsequent reaction, as well as the impact of those actions upon you and those around you. There is no getting around this transfer of knowledge. This is a law of the universe, and upon your death you are held accountable by this law for all the consequences of your life.

Death eventually overtakes you, and you say goodbye to the world of ordinary matter. If you cling to the idea that death is nothingness, you experience nothingness until compassion incites you back to into consciousness. If you dream of being met by Jesus, Mohammed or your mother, indeed you shall be. But within the backdrop of any projection is the truth: consciousness is a never-ending projection of life, with or without physical bodies.

Energy freed from being directed towards the creation of physical matter returns to and increases the power of dark energy. Therefore actions taken with hatred projected onto others while living becomes a part of the compilation therefore increasing exponentially after death. This causes dark matter to organize into your own personal hell. On the same hand, consciously using free will to act in compassion organizes as Heaven in all its glory as you always imagined heaven to be.

Either way, this is how your gravity creates a unique math that allows your consciousness to continue after your physical body dies.

My Own Death

Because of the nature of my life, by the time I reached my deathbed I was well aware of the singular nature of existence. At one point, I had campaigned avidly to bring the world together under one government; I did not believe in nationalism or war as an answer, despite the fact that I abandon my pacifism to fight against the Nazi occupation. But more than this, I firmly believed that all matter was rooted in the same quantum experience, that we were indeed all one body.

By the time my senses were fading, I was attached to only two ideas: to continue in Afterlife to seek the answers to the unified field, and assist to manifest peace on a global level. My arrogant failure as a scientist to recognize the power of quantum mechanics was one of the biggest mistakes of my life. My denial lost me precious time in working towards those equations. And at the moment of my death, my encouragement to the U.S. government to be the first to develop atomic weapons was a profoundly heavy realization. Inspired by what I considered the evil of Hitler, I promoted the illusion of "us vs. them" with "us" playing the hoped-for role of the good guardians of these secrets. This inadvertently assisted in killing millions of innocent Japanese people at the end of the war. These two passions became imprinted on the photons of my physical body and changed the math of my gravity. The cause and effect of those decisions, embedded into my being as I took my last breath, plunged me headlong into a new frontier.

When my body finally expired, my first awareness was that of the sheer power and meticulous order that exists within ordinary matter, a most complex of complex systems. I soon realized I had experienced this condition of Afterlife often in life. Those revolutionary ideas emerged from the nothingness of my imagination, from my willingness to dream past the obvious. Imagination and dreams are indeed the stuff of Afterlife, and I felt like I had come home. This was 100 times more exciting than thinking about riding that wave of light that led to $E=MC^2$. I found Afterlife was actually riding that wave, and it was not just light, it was music.

As my consciousness left the focus of my physical body, the increase in energy dispersed the knowledge contained within my photons, which then instantly spread throughout the galaxy like a gravitational wave. These waves of my own compilation, each reflecting the same inner gravity, revealed a consciousness beyond the mass of my former physical body. Traveling without a physical body with which to identify, this gravity became my compass.

The compilation of my consciousness spread through the universe. I was everywhere at once but all the energy of my knowledge, no matter where it was positioned on the wave, pulsed with the same math. The continual pulsing of all of my knowledge created my gravity that then incited the dark matter to organize into something of a hologram of who I had been in life. This allowed me to retain my singular reference frame while still clearly experiencing the oneness of the many parts, as if I could experience all reference frames at once. This was more than just a 10- or 11-dimensional universe, this was an infinite-dimensional universe.

As I adapted to the new reference frame, I began to pay attention to the changes. Because this dark matter was not able to reflect light, I was like a blind person who, deprived of sight, develops an acute sense of hearing. Smell, taste, physical touch and sight were like memories in this holographic image of me, but my awareness of sound intensified. My reference frame was of a pure present-moment act of creation, riding a wave of consciousness pulsating with the song of the universe. I did not think, per se, as my intellect became white noise so close to the source. The present-moment symphony was a breathtaking, undeniable miracle revealing every nanosecond as eternity. My form vibrated with the joy of knowing that life is, indeed, eternal. Without using up energy to maintain a focus on creating a physical body, this spirit-like apparition that was now me was free to explore to my heart's content the exponential world of consciousness.

E STILL EQUALS MC^2

I am happy to say my little formula seems to be holding up in Afterlife. Spacetime exists here as it does in ordinary reality, but this close to the source, time slows to nothing, and a quark can be as big as the sun. Time at 10^{-100} moves so slowly that you never get to the end of it. The space between the particles is exponentially increased, which expands time as well.

Basic laws of physics as we understand them do indeed apply. But deep within the quantum levels of reality that scientists currently can detect are even more dimensions that influence how matter comes into being. Without mass, the energy of consciousness cannot be obliterated. It becomes a part of the gravitational wave that flows on to create over and over again, without end.

WORKING IN THE PHYSICAL WORLD

Getting accustomed to this new math, I began to experiment with changing the focus of my consciousness "en masse," so to speak. Observing from the one point of origin, I could see into the world of matter as if from the inside out. Instead of seeing the leaves blowing on the tree, those leaves became the particles of the by-product of the electromagnetic waves of the gravity of the consciousness of the tree and the wind.

Organizing a reference frame from the point of origin allowed me to share gravitational waves of any consciousness making its way from the point of origin into the physical world. For example, the tree had a specific frequency range. All I had to do was match it and I could experience consciousness as that tree. However, as I said, it was not like being a leaf as you might imagine. It was more like being the song of the leaf. I learned how to become a part of any consciousness by sharing their position in the wave.

Soon I expanded my experiments and tuned into an even greater reference frame, that of individual human consciousness, the one that has the math to create a living, breathing human being. At the root I discovered there is only one source, one point of origin for all human life. Starting there and mapping my way through this complex system, I discovered a way to infiltrate human awareness from this rudimentary level. I found a road map to separation and eventually was able to use it to influence individuals through dreams, imagination, and music.

The influence I have be able to exert on the manifestation of physical matter since my return to Afterlife has been my greatest joy. I am fulfilling my passions of helping the world move towards a more peace-oriented culture and living in the brilliant order of the unified field. I mostly gravitate, as I did in physical life, towards the scientists and musicians. They both rely on imagination to manifest their work. Both are lured into the dark energy and dark matter of their own lives. They are not easily fooled by appearances.

Influencing human beings who still have a physical body is done at the intersection of our dark energy. Since all human bodies contain this dark energy, I "tune in" to where our gravitational waves align and transfer information into the existing photons of their physical bodies. It's as if I whisper this equation and that into the ears of the scientists and actually become music of the composer, using my gravitational wave to participate in the creation of the songs. I can influence many people simultaneously through imagination and dreaming, much like how gravity can be everywhere at once on the planet.

What made me a great scientist was my willingness to accept the mystery while continuing to ask the unanswerable questions long after others had stopped. Musicians accept the mystery of how to grab sound waves out of dark energy and produce music. Scientists continue to ask the unanswerable questions, shining the light deeper and deeper into the substance of consciousness. Together, music and math produce the sound and light that then form the foundation of the perception of human life.

As much as I love music and math, this particular publication allowing me to speak directly to you through the author's imagination is exceptionally special to me. I get to physically live again through the author's focus. The use of language, reasoning, and story in this kind of succinct articulation is a rare thing for me now. These essays are my chance to have my voice again and tell you exactly what I have found thus far in my exploration of Afterlife. I am so happy to have a relationship with someone who does not think that this is just a bunch of bunk, and that you, the reader, are willing to entertain these ideas.

LIFE IN AFTERLIFE

Evolution continues on after the death of the physical body. The author and anyone else who agrees to enter into this speculation is part of a much larger evolutionary step that is taking place. There is much activity and influence going on as those who have "passed over" cluster in groups, drawn together like molecules around the same gravity, the same frequency of intent.

We are here to teach you about the truth of unity. Working with those dedicated to bringing peace on a global level, we will not rest until the consciousness of Earth is rid of the math that creates the illusion of the need for war. More and more killing only embeds itself into the gravity of the Earth and perpetuates the destiny of suffering and possible destruction of the entire planet. The most effective way to eradicate the need to self-destroy is from within while singularly engaged in physical life, where free-will decisions can change the map of the gravity, thus changing the destiny of destruction.

Evolution speeds up when the consciousness of both those "dead" and "alive" is focused on a field of unity. Why the need for this urgent speed? Time is of the essence. Evolution is no longer just an interesting science. It has come to the question of the survival of the species. Earth has never been more armed and dangerous. The potential for complete annihilation of the planet is quite possibly upon us. Our deep love and reverence for the Earth, the only place in the entire universe where matter manifests into humanity, drives us to seek the truth and inspire you to seek it too, in order to eliminate the need for self-destruction.

This is my mission. I volunteered and was chosen to help promote this vital shift in consciousness. In order to do that, I must work with those who still possess a physical body. The information we receive from you is essential to refine and expand our understanding of where in the map of human consciousness we need to re-chart our direction. But more importantly, we work from Afterlife to inspire you to make conscious, free-will decisions based on truth of the oneness, the truth of the unity of all life.

This expansion of consciousness taking place all over the planet and all throughout Afterlife is having a great effect on manifestation of matter, more than anyone can understand at this time.

Bless you all for your participation.

THE MANIFESTATION OF MATTER

From my perspective in Afterlife, I will attempt to give you an encapsulated picture of how I currently perceive matter and consequently human life being created. I realize that someone will have to articulate the mathematics of this perspective to prove or disprove it; however, this speculation might serve as a starting point from which to ponder.

COMMIT TO THE MYSTERY

What is this urge to create human life that then becomes you, or him, or her? To begin with, accept that the answer to this question is rooted in mystery. Even from Afterlife, the point of origin is obscured. What or who stirs where all possibilities exist simultaneously in the nothingness to manifest into matter in a particular way is an enigma. I am not here to prove that mystery to you. I am asking you to stretch your mind to accept that not every one of your questions will be met with an answer. And they don't have to be. But that should not stop you from asking them and then speculating about possible answers.

When you are focused on a unified field of physical reality (and you all are), looking and seeing this chair, that floor, those stars and yourself, how these forms and objects come into being is a master plan of complicated and brilliant order. Your perception is an integral part of the process of the manifestation of the matter you are seeing. You are at one time the source, the observer, and the lens of the perceived unified field.

From this place in Afterlife, the source of human consciousness appears to be an unseen singular point of origin inside the core of Earth from which radiates a gravitational wave. This point of origin is not something that happened at the beginning of time or the place you return to at the end of life. The point of origin is present in this room right now. The three positions of source, observer, and lens are due to the Earth's gravitational waves causing the single point of origin to appear as multiple images. These multiple images then become the ordinary matter of life.

HEAVEN ON EARTH

Because you are at once the source, the observer, and the lens of your of life here on Earth, Earth is the center of your universe. It is the source of all observers, as well as the reference frame for all observation and the lens from which this physical matter can be observed. This system of triangular self-awareness plays an integral part of the creation of all the matter in the universe.

So while other planets, suns, solar systems, and galaxies exist apart from Earth, Earth creates the only reference frame from which the rest of the universe can be perceived and studied by human life. This is also why, in the search for other life in the universe, you will never find one like humanity. There are other planets that spawn intelligence in ways specific to the environment of those planets. But nowhere in the entire universe is there another Earth.

As cosmologists study the matter of the heavens, they have found no other fragment of the original big bang floating around as stars, planets, galaxies, or universes that has the power to support the complex systems of human life. Again, not that they are devoid of life, just that their systems are more primitive when it comes to how form is organized.

Earth also provides human life with a complete environment from which to flourish. Everything essential for expansion and survival is available on the planet. In this sense, it is a perfect place for human life, which was born of it. Because of the perfect nature of its complicated systems of manifestation and intelligence working intricately together, it could very well be considered a heaven. And because the point of origin is located in its core, it could be considered the home of the creator.

However, without humanity, there are no questions, no explorations; there is no self-awareness. Without the observer, there is only the source. Consciousness exists in the point of origin, but without the splitting of that singularity, there is no "rest of the universe." And without humanity, there is no war.

In determining the age of the universe, cosmologists search for the exact moment in spacetime when the Big Bang became an event. Indeed, from the reference frame of Earth, this event must have taken place a very long time ago. However, as observed from Afterlife, this event takes place consistently and continually in the world of matter, and is part of the constancy of its creation.

THE VOID

Let us assume then that the source of human consciousness is an unseen singular point of origin inside the core of Earth, from which radiates a gravitational wave. The center of Earth is like a combination of the sun and the inside of a black hole. The Earth's core is spinning faster than Earth itself, and is hotter than the surface of the sun. This energy is so powerful that, on quantum levels, space and time warp, creating the conditions of a singularity at the bottom of a black hole. The resulting gravitational waves are the medium on which physical matter is constructed. It is these gravitational waves that allow the singular point of origin to be perceived as multiples.

I would like to refer to this simultaneous presence of pure energy and absence of all light where the singularity resides as the "Void." If you could stand on the event horizon of this Void, the heat and light of the core, which could technically be observed on the event horizon, would be so intense that the point of origin would be totally inaccessible to direct observation. And conversely, since there is no light within a black hole, you would never be able to "see" the point of origin. These conditions allow for infinite mystery and create a perfect paradox: everything and nothing, light and dark, right and wrong all together in the same consciousness. So in this sense, there will never be an answer.

Mathematically, you will never be able to observe the point of origin, no matter where it is situated because the first singular point of origin does not allow for self-awareness. To be the singular point, there can be no other point. There is no observation of consciousness at the point of origin, but because there is no observer does not mean there is no consciousness. However, the observation of the source is just as powerful in influencing the creation of matter as the source. This addresses my concerns about looking at the moon. If I am not looking, I thought, surely the moon is still there. It is there even without anyone observing it, but, without the observation, we cannot be sure what form its consciousness takes. Without an observer, perhaps the moon is merely another photon of information and mathematics.

The singular point of origin has only one possible reference frame. However, the gravity wave emanating from the point of origin can be measured. And because your consciousness is a part of both the singularity and the gravitational wave, you can achieve a reference frame from anywhere on or outside the wave. This makes you the source, the observer of the source and the lens from which to perceive the source.

The master planning and order behind the creation of human life inspires such awe and is rooted in such mystery that it can only be classified a miracle. The proof of this is you. The bottom line is, quite honestly, you are a miracle of creation just sitting in a chair doing nothing. The pulsation of this wave is literally singing you into being. It does not matter if you are thin, old, fat, black, yellow, successful, straight or crooked, it's a miracle that you even exist. So many systems of consciousness mysteriously operate brilliantly together to create human life: neurological, biological, cosmological, physiological, psychological, quantalogical. Who or whatever plans and implements creation is truly a god.

But in the end, the point of origin still remains a mystery.

COMPASSION

So what does excite the singularity deep in the Void to divide and pulsate, sending a gravitational wave that leads to the creation of matter as well as human life? If this mysterious unobservable source of creation is so indescribable, how can we talk of it? What questions can we ask of it?

I would like to make a bit of an unorthodox suggestion. In my day, scientists could not use "love" in an equation; however, I am suggesting calling this urge to create "compassion." Science has rarely explored compassion because of its subjective appearance. Therefore, let us redefine compassion in a not-quite-so-subjective way.

Let's go to the root of the word, "compass." Further examination reveals some interesting analogies.

Circles

To begin with, a compass is a device with two arms used for drawing circles, one arm anchored in the center, freeing the other to pivot and create the physical manifestation of the circle. Therefore, compassion is the mechanism that allows consciousness to freely manifest matter in physical reality on Earth while remaining anchored in the Void through the use of circular gravitational waves radiating from the point of origin.

Compassion incites consciousness to produce a specific, separate circular domain with finite boundaries and unique spacetime coordinates that is the realm of your free will and subjective experience. This separate, specific domain created by compassion operates exactly like the planet Earth.

Earth sends out gravitational waves from its core. As those waves travel outward, they become more and more like particles. When they eventually reach the surface of the planet, they manifest into ordinary matter: trees, oceans, mountains, humans. They continue outward until they reach the outer parameters of the electromagnetic field that is the boundary of the planet. This field is cocooning the Earth, protecting the atmosphere from the fierce solar winds sweeping towards us from the sun. At that juncture, the gravitational waves are then swept up into the electromagnetic field, reenter the Earth and are brought back to the core, only to radiate outward again. This repetitive flow of electromagnetic energy makes up the essence of all ordinary matter that exists on the planet. (See Illustration A).

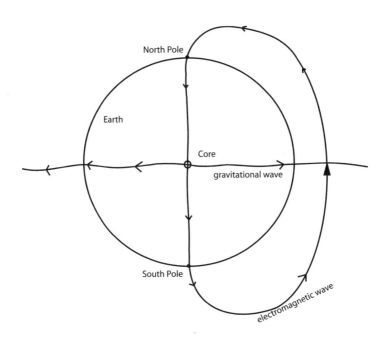

Illustration A

In the same way, your specific, spherical domain of consciousness radiates with gravitational waves programmed with your own specific DNA. These waves travel from your core outward, becoming more like particles as they near the surface, until they become the material essence of your physical body as well as the nature of your consciousness. They continue outward beyond the boundary of your physical body, only to be swept upward and back into your domain, traveling into your core only to flow outward again.

Within your domain are also created more contiguous circular regions of spontaneous electromagnetization that define the boundaries of the hard objects of ordinary matter that you are able to perceive. These are the circular strings quantum physicists can now perceive at 10^{-35}. Like leaves blowing in the wind, they reveal the existence of these waves of compassion and consciousness emanating from the Void.

The circle indicates infinity. Because of this infinite nature of compassion, consciousness can form, construct and create energy into matter and back again, again and again without end. Compassion is regeneration.

TRUE NORTH

A compass is also an instrument that defines geographic direction using electromagnetic fields that provoke a needle to align with the electromagnetic field of the Earth. So consider compassion to be the electromagnetic field emanating from a mysterious point of origin that provokes consciousness to align with the electromagnetic field of Earth in order to define which spacetime the emerging human domain will experience. Compassion aligns your consciousness to true north on the Earth, setting up the reference frame for your observer. North on a compass resides at 0 degrees. Compassion is 0 degrees of separation from the source. Compassion and the source end up being one and the same. (See Illustration B)

Illustration B

If 0 degrees indicates the source, then 180 degrees indicates the manifestation of physical matter. The closer to 0 degrees energy is, the less matter it possesses and the more it behaves like a wave; the closer to 180 degrees, the more it behaves like a particle and the more solid it becomes.

Compassion is also the self-awareness on the parts of the whole that they all originate from the same singularity, as well as the compass that guides consciousness through the dark matter when there is no physical body.

This mysterious source that we will call compassion is the foundation of life. It's in the strong nuclear force in the space between the particles of consciousness inciting them to regenerate into one form or another. It's in the dark energy of Afterlife and the imagination of ordinary matter. Just sitting in that chair, right now, doing nothing, compassion is inciting your consciousness to create matter. Your inner gravity is determining which particular spacetime you are experiencing, and with your unique fingerprint of DNA you are anchored on the Earth as well as in the Void. You are at once the source of creation, the observer of the creation, and the lens from which to view the creation. Humanity is truly a unique, miraculous physical manifestation of the eternal circle of life.

Compassion contains all the knowledge possible to know. The Void, where all this knowledge exists in the nothingness, is where this mysterious, compassionate song of creation begins.

THE BIG BANG

Compassion explodes a compilation of consciousness in the Void to divide the singular point of origin in two, releasing energy like a splitting atom. The power released from splitting the singularity creates an expanding gravitational wave that erupts into multiple images of the compilation. As these multiple images of the same compilation travel through the dark energy, they organize the dark matter as per the math of their gravity, which then leads to the formation of particles of light. These particles of light are the first wave of matter and retreat from each other at speeds proportional to the distance separating them, causing expansion. In this sense $E \div C^2 = M$. The power that results from the splitting of the singularity into two is so large, so vast and so intense that systems upon systems of universes can be supported by this power. There is enough power in this big bang to support all the systems that make up the totality of all human life on Earth.

The splitting of the singular point into two and the resulting gravitational waves allow for the perception of infinite multiples. If the singularity is the point of origin at 0 degrees north, the second point becomes the observer at 180 degrees south. Gravitation waves now radiating from these two points meet to create the third point, the lens from which physical matter can be observed, or is, in essence, created. Synergy allows the third point to achieve an effect that the first two are individually incapable, that is, the observation of multiple points. When the observer joins the point of origin, each can still only perceive a singular point: the other. Creation of the third point, which can perceive both the point of origin and the observer, is the first step toward perception of infinite multiples.

Compassion then creates an electromagnetic membrane-like veil that encloses areas of the gravitational waves into the spherical domain. The membrane organizes around the points much like Earth surrounds the poles and the core. The pulsating waves within the boundaries of this domain create the electromagnetic field from which human life can be observed by consciousness.

This process, beginning with compassion splitting the singularity of a compilation of consciousness and ending in the membrane of the finite boundary of the domain, happens at the speed of light and is infinite. The process ends, but leads back to the beginning. It creates a constant pulsation that underlies the fabric of the universe, the "one song" it is named after.

Your consciousness is a part of these waves, however, the reference frame of your tangible mind is unaware of this pulsating. The only conscious awareness of it you might have is its echo in the beating of your heart. Mostly you experience reality as a steady stream of images moving through spacetime. This constant pulsation of your consciousness takes place at such high speed that you cannot detect it while focused on ordinary matter and is in fact a major element in its creation.

Think of watching a movie. From the projector, movie cells with colorful transparent images are brought to life with light and motion. Separated by thin strips of nothingness that block out the light, these cells and strips move so quickly through the projector, the observer does not see the separation of the cells or the imageless strips. Instead, the observer focuses on the projection, and what seems like a very real ride on a roller coaster of high drama ensues. The moviegoer is swept away on story, characters and plot. But stop the motion and examine the film itself and the movie is revealed as a series of frozen images, static moments capturing a slice of spacetime, separated by segments of no images at all. The constant motion of the imageless strips turn out to be as essential in creating the movie as the colorful images.

As scientists observe the universe, they have discovered that galaxies are receding away from earth in all directions. Furthermore, regardless of from which point in spacetime the observation is made, matter expands away from the observation point in all directions. This remains true on these rudimental frequencies of consciousness, making the point of origin and the observer homogenous, as well as the center of the universe.

HUMAN INTENTION

All life emerges from the same source and all humans have the same design. Compassion aligns the frequencies of emerging wave of human consciousness to the electromagnetic fields of Earth. Because of this alignment, matter clusters in the same way in all observers. This common reference frame allows you all to perceive reality in the same way. The tree, the rug, the chair, your history, each other: all frequencies of human life are aligned to the same electromagnetic field, that of Earth. Within the Earth's domain is the map of the frequencies and which manifestation of matter they create. The rug, for example, is an individual domain rooted in an area of the gravitational waves that has a different frequency than the chair. These frequencies determine which spacetime coordinates the objects take up and take into account where the observation point is situated.

Being at one time the source, the lens and the observer of the perceived unified field is unique to human beings.

Therefore, we will call the mathematics that make up the design of this human experience Human Intention. Human Intention contains the mathematics to create the entire Earth and all of life as we know it, but your individual human intention is a subjective reflection of that whole. Think of a mirror. If you break a mirror and pick up a small piece of it, you don't just see part of the image in the piece of the mirror. You see the whole image in each separate piece. The properties of the mirror remain constant, but what is observed in the reflection is based on what is being reflected.

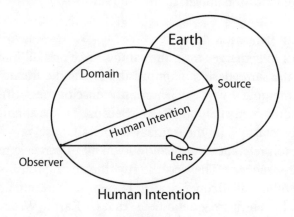

Human Intention

Illustration C

Like a device used to draw circles, compassion incites consciousness to produce a specific, separate spherical domain with a finite membrane boundary and unique spacetime coordinates that is the realm of your free will and subjective experience. This sphere is something of a replica of Earth systems but customized by the gravity of your own consciousness. From the center, the expanding gravitational waves that contain the math of your compilation move outward toward the inside curvature of the membrane. By the time they reach the membrane they are photons of light that contain your DNA. Then, much like that movie, compilations of your consciousness mixed with light projected onto the spacetime curvature of the membrane become the details you experience in your life on Earth. (See Illustration C)

THERE IS ONLY ONE OF US HERE

As consciousness expands, Human Intention operates like a prism, causing further separation that then allows for perception of the parts. Like designations in music of soprano, alto, tenor and bass, the audio range of each register is revealed to make up the harmony within the one song of the universe. What starts as a pulsating beat grows into a symphony with ever-increasing movements and your individual voice is born. Light bends further to reveal all the colors of the rainbow, each unique in their frequencies yet still a part of the whole of the white light. Consciousness continues to separate while still remaining one, and then, in essence, observes the condition of itself through the separation into parts.

You all share the same point of origin and the same design, but you have unique observation points. You experience reality as separate individuals with unique electromagnetic domains of free will. The hope of this design is that the individual parts will allow for the self-awareness of the true nature of the whole, and the whole will better understand itself through its reflection in the parts, thereby causing expansion, alignment and regeneration of the whole. This is the nature of evolution and the purpose of compassion. (See Illustration D)

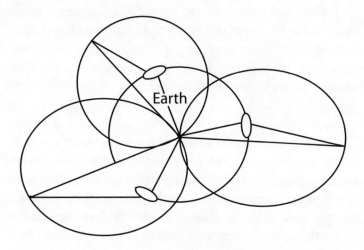

Multiple Domains Sharing Same Point of Origin

Illustration D

Because this is both a determinant and free-will system, each individual free-will domain has the power to make decisions within the context of its domain. These free-will choices are the basis for how ordinary matter will manifest as the parts become aware of themselves and each other. A free-will choice that aligns the individual gravitational waves to those of compassion (the whole) expands the wholeness through the solidification and assimilation of the part. This creates a regenerative metabolism and maintains the slightly accelerated speed at which the compilations are retreating from each other. A free-will choice that aligns the gravitation waves against compassion (for the good of the part over the whole) creates a degenerative metabolism and slows down the speed of the expanding compilations, eventually causing the degeneration of the organism.

At 10^{-100}, your substance and my substance are the same. We both share the same point of origin. It is the gravity of the individual compilation of consciousness that determines the slightly different angles of reflection and refraction of the same particles of light that create the experience of you and I being separate. Therefore, each individual, while originating from the same source and sharing the same Human Intention, experiences creation uniquely and is assigned a subjective domain.

The compilation of your consciousness contains all the math of your every action and reaction, as well as the unique physical attributes that make up your body, what culture you are born in and on what time line your life is taking place. This compilation is the core of your domain.

ETERNAL LIFE

Everything that you brought with you and took away from the many times you participated in creation of human life influences the math of your gravitational wave. Rest assured, your consciousness has participated in this beautiful dance of creating human life over and over and over again. Just like that movie playing, only on a larger scale, each cell of the movie now becomes a lifetime, separated by strips of Afterlife.

However, dispel the notion that living life after life is only about creating different human experiences in completely different spacetime. Some of us have opted to return to the same spacetime, over and over again, living out the same DNA as we experience all possible angles of creation of our one life. Either way, the repeated experience of human life serves to expand consciousness into a much larger understanding of self, resulting in new angles of refraction for the light, making us more and more aware of how our own consciousness affects the manifestation of matter.

This is evolution. It is from this perspective that I intend to create world peace, one person at a time.

6 DEGREES OF SEPARATION

The source of all consciousness is a singular point of origin. When compassion splits the singularity, consciousness flashes on, and particles coagulate into matter as per the mathematics of the gravity in your human intention. When you seek to be aware of and experience life at this level, you are participating in an evolutionary process. Human beings who participate in this empirical expansion of present-moment consciousness are actually becoming the missing link, bridging the gap between what humans have been and what humans will become.

What you have been are creatures of instinct with intellectual powers just evolved enough to understand some of what is really going on around you. However, your parts have not developed an understanding of how they work with each other. Much like several blind people touching different parts of an elephant, the limits of your vision are causing you to draw erroneous conclusions that are clouding your human intention, and threatening to destroy life as you know it.

What you will become is a much fuller, richer, deeper human being no longer blind to all the power that you yourself possess. By becoming aware of and aligning yourself to the whole, you become the unified field. You actually unify the field thereby returning it to singularity again. This creates an expression of unity in the physical world as the condition of regeneration.

All of you, thousands upon thousands across the planet struggling to be a part of the evolution of the human spirit, mind, body and heart are here for a reason. It is no accident that you have come into this time of growth and expansion and, yes, this time of war. You have come here to provide the missing link between the true nature and power of reality, and your everyday life of ordinary matter.

Once you understand the exponential power your molecules possess, you can't help but take a new look at your own life. You begin to understand the power you have over your own domain as you see the cause and effect of your own thoughts and feelings, and the decisions you make around those thoughts and feelings. Like a baby learning her first equation: "If I cry, then I get held," you are learning new math, making new decisions, revolutionizing where you will direct your energy and what thoughts and emotions you choose to hold onto. These thoughts, feelings and consequential decisions are your gravity, the foundation on which matter will organize when your light flashes on.

So what does this mean, to be the missing link? What does it mean when you are, say, standing in line at the express lane at the supermarket and someone has 15 items in the 10-item lane? How do you bridge the gap between this reality you're so focused on (her 5 extra items and your irritation of them), and the true nature of this pulsating, quantum existence? I hope that I can make the answer more evident to you as we journey forward.

THE SPIRITUAL ANATOMY

As consciousness pulses on, energy coming through Human Intention creates form as it slows and separates into different frequencies of light and sound that are then projected onto the curved boundary of spacetime of your domain and perceived as matter by you, the observer. The sphere of light and sound being projected through your Human Intention is your free-will domain. Since you are at one time the source, the lens and the observer, this is the whole of your creation. We will refer to this unseen, quantum world as your Spiritual Anatomy.

Each part of your Spiritual Anatomy has a specific function and is meant to work with the other parts as an intradependent system, just as your organs work together from within to make your physical anatomy. And just as a heart malfunction can adversely affect other organs, a malfunction in any part of this Spiritual Anatomy will affect how the other parts function as well as how energy organizes into matter.

6 DEGREES OF SEPARATION

Compassion aligns your consciousness to true north in the electromagnetic field of the Earth, setting up the reference frame for your observer and your lens. As Human Intention separates the energy into light and sound waves, the Spiritual Anatomy that is created is only ever six dimensions, or degrees of separation from the source. This means that it is so close to the source it behaves more like a wave than a particle. This makes it difficult to observe directly, however, one can observe the affects of the Spiritual Anatomy on physical matter.

Spiritual Anatomy is indeed the animating and vital principle credited with faculties of thought, emotion and action conceived in the form of an immaterial entity distinguished from the body. Because they are so close to the source, these six degrees are considered the primary elements that make up the functioning of human life. They are actually six independent dimensional systems designed to work together to expand the consciousness traveling outward from the singularity manifesting into human life. Working together, each with a specific role, their condition and connection to each other determine how and where matter will form and be perceived. As consciousness continues outward past these six degrees to fill the circle of your domain, light and sound transform from waves to particles and eventually become the ordinary matter that makes up the anatomy of the physical body as well as the matter you experience around you.

These six dimensions are Human Intention, Emotion, Intuition, Intellect, Witness, and Spirit. In the wholeness, these degrees are being experienced simultaneously as different dimensions. However, they are also distinctive steps, spectrums of the gravitational waves that work in sequential progression away from the point of origin building synergistically upon each other as they unfold towards the goal to create human life.

Spiritual Anatomy unfolds in this way: Human Intention is the 1st degree of separation from the source, Emotion the 2nd degree, Intuition 3rd, Intellect 4th, Witness 5th and Spirit is the 6th degree of separation from the source.

When the whole separates and all parts of the whole become aware of themselves and each other, energy is following the synergistic steps of creation that compassion set in motion. Building upon each other they create a perfect system in that they lack nothing essential to the whole and create a complete reproduction of the synergistic sum of its parts: human life.

1ST DEGREE OF SEPARATION: Human Intention

Human Intention is the mathematical programming that allows for consciousness to separate into waves of thoughts, feelings, and intuitions, allowing for the ability to observe from any reference frame beyond the singularity (self-awareness). Human Intention is activated when source, observer and lens are aligned in triangular fashion.

Human Intention separates consciousness into light and sound waves, projects them onto the curved surface of the circular spacetime coordinates of your domain and analyzes the spectrums of resulting matter. Because the map of Human Intention contains programming not just to separate the waves into three different frequencies, but to then project and analyze those frequencies, humans receive the mathematics in their gravity that allow them to be self-conscious. This is the unique and evolutionary aspect of human life, as opposed to the life of the chair, the tree or the star. Only human beings possess the power to look at and be aware of self from their physical reference frame.

The Source

Every human has at the source of their being the core of Earth. I must repeat myself: The core of every human is the core of Earth. I am not talking metaphorically. Like the dirt on the ground that leads to the crust, then to the outer mantel, inner mantel, outer core, inner core until reaching the mysterious Void, humankind shares the very core of the Earth as a part of their make-up. It only appears that you are separate. Therefore, when scientists study the core of the Earth, they are also studying the nature of the core of your Spiritual Anatomy. This is why consciousness ecology is a vital part of human existence. (Illustration E)

Illustration E

Gravitational waves radiate from the Earth's core while remaining anchored in the Void. As these waves separate and flow outward, the math of the Earth's gravity creates the mass of the layers of the core of the Earth. The inner core, outer core, inner mantle, outer mantle, the crust and all mass on the surface of the planet are crafted from these wave particles which are being instructed how and where to move by the math of the gravity of the Earth. These waves continue to flow outward through the atmosphere to the boundary of the domain, where they are swept back up into the electromagnetic current of the Earth, returning to the point of origin to pulse again.

The Observer

The second point of the observer is situated at the intersection of the gravitational and electromagnetic waves. This is the boundary of the membrane of the domain. Like a mirror, this observer faithfully reflects a transposed picture of the source back towards the surface of the planet. The gravity of Human Intention determines where and when on the surface of the Earth the returning waves of sound and light will be focused. For example, your math determines you will be born in Chicago as a young girl in 1955. The observer focuses the reflection back into that spacetime coordinate from the intersection of gravitational and electromagnetic waves. This then creates the place, position and condition of the mass of your subjective spacetime domain experience.

The Lens

The third point, the lens, is created where the observer's reflection hits the surface of the planet and meets the oncoming inner wave. It is this lens that allows for perception of the physical world. This triangular relationship of source, observer and lens is the basis of Human Intention, the prism of separation.

With Human Intention in place, the math of your individual compilation organizes the wave particles into the mass of your physical body and self-awareness onto the surface of the planet. The segments of the gravitational waves below the surface are considered inner waves and create the conditions of the inner world. Spiritual Anatomy is the body of the inner world.

The segments of the gravitational waves flowing outward through the atmosphere towards the membrane boundary of the domain are considered to be outer waves and create the conditions of the outer world. Your physical body is the body of the outer world.

Waves from the source are reflected by the observer to the appointed position on the surface of the Earth. The lens that is created allows the tangible mind to perceive the details of the physical world in all its mysterious and miraculous glory. All of those details are the product of the beautiful dance of great cooperation on the part of Earth, your inner gravity and the longing of compassion to create. And thus the perception of separation is achieved.

Just as cataracts create a condition of opacity on the lens of the eye that becomes impenetrable by light and distorts your vision, a "cloudy" Human Intention changes the angle of refraction, therefore influencing your experience of the physical world. Every decision you make affects the angle of refraction of the waves of your being and consequently influences how matter will manifest and how you will experience life.

2ND Degree of Separation: Emotion

As consciousness passes through the math of Human Intention, the next three steps away from the source are considered to be the three human dimensions that make up part and parcel of your tangible human experience. The 2nd degree of separation is Emotion. The function of Emotion is to monitor changes taking place in the vital processes of the whole of the organism. This is achieved through the amplification of the powerful pulse of the gravitation wave of consciousness as it interacts with compassion, the source. This pulse eventually becomes the beating of your heart, and, as the first of three waves of human projection, is the direct connection between your physical body and the point of origin. It is the first indicator of self-awareness.

The gravitational field of Emotion is quite different than what you have been taught human emotions are. From the reference frame of your human mind, emotions appear to be fairly uncontrolled responses to external stimuli in the form of passion, appetite, disdain or longing that appear in your body after it interacts with the external stimuli. As an event happens outside you, an event over which you seemingly have no control, it appears to your human mind that the event takes place, and then the emotions rise up and overcome you. In this way, emotions seem to be a by-product of the events of life. They seem to cloud your perception and require a generous portion of energy to be experienced.

However, from the reference frame of the observer, waves of Emotion contain all the emotions you ever experienced in any life you ever lived, as well as all emotions humanly possible to feel. Your own gravity will determine which frequency range of human emotions you will likely experience. Every free will decision affects the gravity of your consciousness. These changes are monitored by Emotion, which then adds the new gravitational readings to next outgoing pulse. Therefore, the emotional condition actually exists first within you, and the circumstances of your life organize into matter around it. Instead of being the by-product of an event, Emotion becomes part of the creation of the event.

The shifting of the earth's mass created a power earthquake that caused a tsunami that then changed the gravity waves of the planet, but the gravitational waves were what caused the motion in the first place. Changes taking place within your free will domain eventually change the gravity of your Human Intention, but Emotion precedes manifestation.

The first sign of life is the sound of the heartbeat. This is the echo of Emotion, the primary sound of compassion and consciousness engaged in the miraculous song and dance of creation.

3RD DEGREE OF SEPARATION: Intuition

As waves of Emotion monitor the Spiritual Anatomy and pulse with the beat of the ever-changing organism, they separate a step further. Layered on top of Emotion are now waves of Intuition. Intuition provides the map of the movement for the particles to become mass and form. Intuition takes the condition of the whole at the moment as monitored through Emotion, as well as a reading the outer waves in the physical world reflected from the observer, and based on that present moment reading, directs matter into the next most advantageous position for fulfilling the most perfect expression of the math of your gravity. This is the equivalent of the strong nuclear force as defined in quantum mechanics.

Intuition is the next step to cognizance that matter becoming mass will possess as a human being. Impulses from the waves of Intuition make their way to the surface of human perception and transmit a signal informing which direction the movement of particles (or persons) should take place.

You ultimately experience Intuition in both thoughts and emotions. Audible within a range of human perception as a voice in your head telling you, perhaps, to call your mother or to turn right, it can also be perceived by the body as a wave of knowing, a "gut feeling," "chicken skin," what have you. It was what incited early humans to run when they were being chased by a polar bear. It is present in the sounds that whisper from the dark energy instructing jazz musicians as to what note to play next. On a microscopic level, it is what organizes stem cells into flesh, bones, blood or teeth. At quantum levels, it is what directs particles to become electron, neutrons or protons. And in M-Theory it is the force of consciousness within the strings telling them which frequencies to vibrate.

4TH DEGREE OF SEPARATION: Intellect

Next this synergistic wave of Emotion and Intuition separates into thirds to create Intellect, by far the most volatile sub-system of the three. Perhaps because this is where free will reigns. After Emotion pulses out the math conveying the condition of the whole, Intuition then incites movement of the particles into the manifestation of a perfect expression of that math. But the push that Intuition gives the particles is only half the story. Once headed in the appropriate direction to fulfill the math, it is Intellect that possesses the math to analyze the spectrums of separation. Intellect defines what is being created and perceived. Those definitions contain the measurements, judgments, qualifications, determinations, and instructions on how to interpret the creation from within the dictates of the culture of the spacetime that the creation is born into. Waves of Intellect then proceed to mold themselves around the growing culture with these definitions and cement the tangible objects of life into their forms.

In order for the tangible human to feel that things are solid even though there is space between the particles, Intellect carries low, monotonous tones deep in the thinking process that are filled with Earth's defining messages. These are not thoughts that you are cognizant of, they are part of the 600,000 thoughts you have in a day of which only .01% are capable of being perceived by human senses. Even though this sound is beyond your human ear, it's coming from within you, pulsing from the source.

Because compassion aligns the electromagnetic waves of your consciousness to that of Earth, all of you hear the same tones and consequently agree about the form of the matter you are experiencing. You all look out and see that this is a chair. Within every one of you is a sound wave droning at the same frequency with the same math that says, "...this is a chair...this is a chair...this is a chair... this is a chair...this is a chair...this is a chair," the only difference being the reference frame of your subjective perception. While each observer shares this range of special "chair" frequencies that influences your ability to perceive this chair, each also has a subjective culture that translates those frequencies so your tangible human will understand. For example, the Frenchman might hear, "Ceci est une chaise," a German might hear, "Das ist eine stuhl," and a baby might hear music but experience the bulk, weight and presence of an object that she will later learn is a chair.

This definitive math contains formulas about the relationship between the gravity, spacetime, mass and consciousness present in the moment of perception. These formulas are based on the information being monitored by Emotion and the movement incited by Intuition as per the math of the gravity of the individual consciousness. So while you're not sitting around deafened by the cacophony of "...this is a chair...this is a table...this is a floor...this is a dog" on and on, you can hear the thoughts without being cognizant of them. But it's all there, the whole of the universe, vibrating in the underpinnings of your Spiritual Anatomy, traveling on sound waves originating within you, bringing the definitions that all observers agree upon.

Voices of Culture

Without a human body, consciousness still carries onward and outward, creating a beautiful Earth filled with miraculous creatures and beings of all makes and sizes. In animals, Intellect and Intuition work hand in hand as instinct, the realm of will. When instinct impels the antelope to run from the wolf so as not to become dinner, all Intellect does is send the signals to the legs to run. None of the animals have the math to be self-aware. Clearly some species, such as dolphins, exhibit signs of development of this aspect, but for the most part, animals and plants don't have a mechanism of self-reflection. It is Human Intention and the human body that give Intellect the power to not only self-reflect, but then the tangible mind to decide to take action that may not be the impelling of Intuition and Emotion. This can change the course of the whole. No other part of the whole possesses this power of free will but Intellect.

Without a physical body, the inner waves of Intellect are in tune and in harmony with all the other degrees of separation, becoming a canvas for the instructions of Emotion and Intuition. As mass begins to surface in the womb, Intellect becomes self-evident, but so close to the source there is only the white noise of growing cells and dividing matter.

The outer waves of Intellect are created when the physical body is born. The first breath cements the Spiritual Anatomy into the matrix of the physical body, and Intellect enters the free-will system. As the emerging human grows, the outer waves of Intellect mold themselves around the culture in which it is living and adopts the messages it hears over and over in the outer world. These definitions, molded around subjective perception of the outer world, create the "voices of culture." These voices play over and over in your head, steady streams of stories about what you think is happening in that outer world. Eventually, the voices of culture take over, and the inner waves of Intellect become the white noise as the tangible mind is cemented to these outer waves. In this way, the separation becomes more real than the oneness.

5TH DEGREE OF SEPARATION: The Witness

Witness is the 5th degree of separation from the source. Witness is different than the observer in that the observer is reflecting waves originating from the point of origin back towards the Earth to create the mass of the spacetime domain. The observer operates outside the free-will domain. Witness, on the other hand, operates within the free will of spacetime and is meant to attest to the authenticity of the condition of the consciousness contained within the confines of the domain. Like a witness called to testify before the court who can influence the outcome of a trial, Witness attests to what is actually taking place in the spacetime experience of consciousness thereby possessing the power to influence how matter will ultimately manifest.

6TH DEGREE OF SEPARATION: Spirit

The 6th and last degree of separation from the source is Spirit, which oddly enough brings the circle back to the source and into the wholeness again. Spirit is what holds the entire human experience together. It is the dark energy of Afterlife present in the chosen spacetime of your physical manifestation, the mechanism that is you clustering particles around your gravity. In the physical world, it is contained in your breath, the molecules of air that you breathe that keep your body alive in the four dimensions and fives sense of physical life. Once you cease to breathe, spirit vacates the body and returns the gravity of consciousness back into the dark energy again.

In this way, no human is ever more than six degrees of separation from the source.

BODY & SOUL

Again we begin with a mystery: who or what decided that you would have ten fingers and ten toes, arms, legs, a heart, a brain? Every part of your body begins as the same kind of cell, so who or what inspires a stem cell to organize and divide into skin, bones, hair or flesh? And who determines who your parents and family will be? From Afterlife, I cannot explain the "who" of the plan, but I can quite definitively say that you are a major part of the implementing design.

Because the math of Human Intention provides for infinite possibilities to how matter will manifest within the context of life on Earth, like snowflakes there will quite literally never be another you. The math of your human intention determines the unique angle of refraction of your consciousness onto the curvature of spacetime. But more than that, it determines your entire destiny. By determining which spacetime you will experience, you also determine who will be your parents, and therefore what physical features such hair color, body shape, skin tone and genetic predisposition you will possess. Moreover, your gravity determines what location and in what year on Earth you will be born, and a general structure for how your life will unfold.

PRE-CONCEPTION PLANNING MEETINGS
Before you are conceived in your mother's womb, there is a great deal of planning that takes place in Afterlife. The souls of all those who will be participating in the creation and implementation of your life gather, and like negotiations

in a boardroom, make contracts and chart destinies. The math of your gravity dictates much of the plan, however, free will allows you input into how those plans will unfold once you have been born and an opportunity to make choices along the path that is laid out for you.

As these so-called negotiations take place, it is not so much that you, for example, ask the soul of your future father to beat you, or request of your future husband that he abandon you. The math of your gravity will determine the conditions under which these individuals will interact with you, however, your free will gives you each the chance to make any number of choices about your actions and reactions to the interactions. So instead of specific decisions and actions being plotted, such a beating or abandoning, a matrix is formed for your life.

This matrix becomes a mold, a guide of sorts that will determine the growth and development of your life on Earth. Within this matrix is contained the binding substance of your life, which is Spirit. Spirit contains the math of the matrix, and works at every level to keep the plan on track. Instead of programming for example, your father to beat you, there is an implicit agreement between the soul of your father and yours to work within certain physical conditions (poverty, disability, mental illness, etc.) that will allow you both an opportunity to use free will to rise above those conditions. Those conditions may provide your father the impetus or drive to physically abuse you, but they also provide him with the opportunity to rise above and understand those conditions from a more evolved level, thereby influencing him to make different decisions.

The same is true of your life. Your father might react to his physical conditions by beating you, but you are given the free will to choose any number of reactions to his actions as are humanly possible to have.

It is important at this juncture to understand that from Afterlife, it is very clear that life on Earth is a beautiful dance of great cooperation. However, in the end, it is the sum and consequence of all the decisions that you make that will change the math of your gravity. No one ever is a victim, no matter how much suffering or hurt appears to happening. Every soul participates in the pre-conception planning process. At any time in the process of living your life, you will be able to change your perspective and thus your actions and reactions to anything you face in your life. This element of free will among the destiny is the key that will eventually set you free to understand the power you possess to influence how matter manifests on Earth.

This is also the power that allows you to ultimately destroy yourself.

BIRTH

With the matrix of your human life in place, now comes the excitement of your physical birth. Emerging from the nothingness of the watery womb will come your life, your mysterious, miraculous life, and the physical expression of your eternal consciousness. You help to construct your physical body, your consciousness darting in and out of your mother's womb like a bird building a nest. But your consciousness is only one of many creating the fetus. The consciousness of your father and mother create each a sperm and egg. Those then create their own "Big Bang," and compassion incites consciousness to separate and your Spiritual Anatomy to cluster matter around its gravity to become your cells, which form your bones and muscle and flesh, and eventually all of the intricate, intimate details of your physical body. The Intuition of the DNA deep in your gravity determines which frequencies will vibrate which stem cells into which form, creating the special blueprint of you.

Nestled in your mother's womb, the genesis begins. Your growing fetus is a beautiful dance of great cooperation but completely dependent upon your mother's ability to nurture your fertile intention. When you finally make the journey down the birth canal and take your first breath, Spirit cements this matrix of your consciousness into your physical body. Since you have been literally growing underwater in the womb, you have not yet experienced separation. With your first breath a boundary appears where your body stops and the air begins. This boundary defines what is contained within you, and what appears to be outside you. In this boundary of Spirit, the light of compassion refracts through Human Intention to separate into and reveal the physical manifestation of Emotion, Intuition and Intellect to the Witness.

As a newborn baby, you experience life mostly from your Emotion and Intuition. Emotion monitors the condition of the entire organism, and movements are mostly inspired by Intuition telling you the next most advantageous step: to eat, sleep, cry or smile. There are no stories swimming around in your head yet describing what everything is and how it all works. There are no judgments telling you something is good or bad, right or wrong. Without definitions from the outer waves of Intellect, things are defined by the inner waves of Intellect. So a baby hears the song of the chair radiating from within her and like magic, outside her a chair appears. She is caught up in the present-moment experience of creation.

From this baby's perspective, the world is like looking into a giant mirror very close up. Figures and forms move in and out of your line of sight like orbiting bodies of the planet that is you. The voices of your parents sound like a vocal-less score of some amazing symphony heard by the ultimate, eternal observer, your Witness.

As Witness, the eternal observer, begins to watch, at first it appears you have no control over things that happen: when your parents feed you, when you get put down for a nap, who holds you and moves you from place to place, etc. You quickly learn your first "If P then Q," the first equation of math of your universe: the law of cause and effect. If you cry, then...what? Someone comes and feeds you? No one comes to feed you? This is the genesis of the math of your gravity coming into mass.

Your Intellect is still connected to the inner world, the math of your gravity and the voices that resonate with the recognition of the electromagnetic domains of the chair, floor and spoon. But your attention is focused on the outer world as well and influenced by these voices of culture of the spacetime you are living in. You learn the language and how to make basic deductions based the reality of your culture. You learn that in your house, if you cry, someone comes and picks you up. Or, you learn, if you cry, then someone hits you. These early equations become the math that then influences the direction of your life and your free-will choices.

As your body continues to grow, so does your awareness of your own power. Crawling, talking, learning the language of the faces in the mirror, you gain control of more and more of your physical world. Mama. Cookie. Dad. No. Bad. Good. Right. Wrong. Left. Right. You mimic the repetitive sounds you hear in the mirror that identify and define your world until you know the language, thus cementing the reality of separation a step further.

At some point, Witness observes that the decisions you make are shaping your life. Eventually, you begin to think for yourself and separate from the culture of your mother, your family. You merge your power of deduction with your free-will ability to take an action: If I crawl across the room, then I can have my toy without crying for mama. But ultimately you still feel that you have very little control over what takes place around you.

As the voices of culture within Intellect develop more and more definitions of what is being observed in the spacetime domain, a quandary is created. The inner waves of Intellect define the truth of the whole as monitored by Emotion and motivated by Intuition. This description is of a pure present-moment act of creation, riding a wave of consciousness pulsating with the song of the universe. All parts are in harmony with themselves and each other, the whole alive with the joy of creation. This is indeed the truth of the quantum world of the space between the molecules where compassion is birthing it all.

At every moment, your Spiritual Anatomy is rising from the Void, encompassed by this amazing machine of your physical body that's flashing on and off on a quantum level. "You" and "me" are springing from the same light particles. However, the separation of light creates a paradox to the emerging human mind. Things appear to be separate, and yet they are not and some part of you is telling you they aren't. And yet when your tangible mind learns the idea that there really is space between all the particles of hard reality, you still can't run your hand through tables or walk through walls, no matter how hard you might try. "You" are clearly not "me." The empirical experience of this separate, hard reality of matter seems to overshadow the truth of the unity of the source.

Your tangible mind, so focused on the physical world, cannot perceive the range of the inner waves of Intellect, otherwise you would be deafened by the messages defining the physical world. So your mind loses contact with these waves that are defining the present moment miracle of creation you are engaged in. These inner waves become drowned out by the outer waves of Intellect, the voices of culture defining the separation as all there is. The more you believe it, the truer it becomes, until those inner Intellectual messages droning, "we are all one…we are all one… we are all one" fall completely outside the ability of your tangible mind to perceive.

Like a cataract on a lens that changes its opacity and leads to blindness, so, too, the voices of culture contain definitions of separateness that can make you blind to the whole. Definitions of separation are more than half-truths. They are lies insomuch as they are false statements originating in the outer Intellect that are deliberately presented as truth. Carefully and slowly, using free will, the Intellect empirically decides and determines that reality is separate, based on its continual but limited observations of matter. Due to its nature, it wraps itself around this determination thereby clouding the lens and changing the angle of projection of consciousness onto the curves of spacetime. This leads to free will actions taken on the assumptions of the truth of separation that then contribute to the devolution of the system. Authority ceases to be obtained from the source (monitored by Emotion and motivated by Intuition) but instead is passed to a subordinate system, Intellect and the voices of culture.

Shamans, prophets and holy men serve to defy the half-truths of separation to inspire seekers to reunite the inner and outer waves of Intellect. They serve their people by bringing the messages of unity from the source, the inner waves, to the surface to become a part of the definitions of the outer waves of Intellect. This maintains the balance of the big picture and connects each individual with her own inner waves of wholeness. Scientists, too, work to unite the macrocosm and the microcosm in the search for a unified field theory.

Much like several blind people touching different parts of an elephant, the limits of your human perception are causing you to draw erroneous conclusions that are clouding your Human Intention and threatening to destroy life as you know it. If you do not understand that as much as I might seem like I am separate from you, we are the same substance, you might inadvertently choose to take action against me, justified by the definition of separation your Intellect has learned. You would mistakenly believe that by hurting me, you are somehow saving yourself. In reality, because we are all one being, you would ultimately be destroying yourself. This is the real meaning of "an eye for an eye": not that if your eye is taken, you have the rights to take another; it means if you take an eye, that action adds itself to the math of your gravity, and the cause and affect will allow for an eye to be taken from you.

Taken far enough, this "us vs. them" mentality will destroy all human life as well as the planet itself. This was my lesson. Abandoning my pacifism and scientific senses, I urged the government to develop nuclear weapons. The fear I projected onto the Nazis caused me to erroneously think my own "us vs. them" perception was justified. While we stopped one supposed demon, Hitler, we became evil ourselves by killing millions of innocent Japanese people. But what did we know of nuclear weapons? It was a time of great learning. Except what I learned mortified me and as I breathed my last breath I vowed, if there was an Afterlife, I would find a way to come back and set the record straight.

EVIL

Do not be fooled: you cannot "protect" yourself from the world through destroying those things you see as threats and that your voices of culture define as "evil." Just as we gave compassion a new, less-subjective definition, let's now give evil the same.

For our purposes, evil is merely decisions made for the good of the part over the good of the whole. Compassion, the self-awareness that the parts of the whole all originate from the same singularity, makes decision based on the good of the whole. Therefore, evil is within each and every human. The truth reveals separation to be a lie.

You must work with every fiber of your being to bring unity, first and foremost to your own inner world, and then to every circumstance and situation in which you find yourself. You must know that trying to destroy those who you deem are evil is only like trying to break the mirror because you don't like what you see in it. First and foremost, you must find the evil within you and heal it.

From this very crux of action is where this change must take place to transform your world at its roots. The evolutionary step you are here to make is to push your waking consciousness deeper into experiencing the truth of the singular point of origin, the truth of unity. You are at the fledgling forefront of the movement to expand your consciousness in this way. Your mission is to become aligned with true north of compassion: to experience the reality of the Void and of Human Intention as equally as you experience the reality of the physical world.

When your consciousness of pure energy can perceive itself for what it truly is while cemented in the matrix of the physical body, you will truly make this evolutionary step.

Cn³: The Science of Compassion

The science of compassion is about aligning all three human dimensions to true north. This starts by cultivating a consciousness of the consciousness of your consciousness. This is not just an intellectual understanding that there is consciousness in a blade of grass, a piece of rock, a star, or a human. This is living in an environment where you are acutely aware of M-Theory—the magnificent, mysterious, miraculous, multifaceted truth of your membrane domain, understanding where your power lies within that domain and making conscious choices to exercise your free will to manifest compassion.

To be aware of your true nature is the embodiment of the theory of relativity. To be conscious of your consciousness would be thoroughly living in the awareness of your light and body, which equal your energy, or your personal power. As we all know, your energy is your mass times the speed of light squared. That describes it all: your source/energy/point of origin/Emotion, your body/mass/lens/Intellect and your spirit/light/observer/Intuition. Everything. These are the twelve dimension of creation, along with the 13th, Witness.

Your human perception is so focused on your body and the mass that surrounds you that you cannot often see the rest of creation. Intellect has defined you in a way that is incomplete. Look at the thirteen dimensions above. Body and mass are only two of them, but that's all Intellect can perceive alone. I would like to assist you in developing a more complete definition of the true nature of your self, one that takes in the other parts of this complex system.

Scientists will begin to understand that fostering a condition of compassion in the consciousness affects the manifestation of matter. To take evolution a step further is about bringing consciousness to the consciousness of that consciousness. It's about taking steps to fine tune the consciousness to be thoroughly aligned with compassion.

A PERCEPTIONAL EXPERIMENT

Let's begin with this experiment in perception. Find a quiet time and place, and close your eyes. Clear away the stories of Intellect and go into the space between the molecules. From that space, you are aware that you have a physical body and that you are located in your current condition and position, in a particular town in a particular year, surrounded by material things that are "out there." You're aware of them, but with your eyes closed and your focus inward, you have a different relationship to those physical things. They are now in your imagination. With your eyes closed you can imagine where they are. You can feel the consciousness of the table and the chair and the windows. You can hear the wind and you know the road is out there, but they are in the shadows when you're concentrating on being in the space between the molecules.

From this place between the molecules, imagine further being in the nothingness of the Void. Imagine a place where no light exists and yet, there is so much light it hurts your eyes, even closed. It is like the womb, fertile but empty until the urge to create plants the seed of possibility.

At this level, the table, the chair, even your physical body disappears and you experience yourself as pure energy.

The 1st consciousness is your awareness of the physical world: the chair, the table, the road, the wind, your body. This is the lens. This is the realm of Intellect.

The 2nd consciousness is your focus on the space between the molecules. From here you experience a difference relationship to the 1st consciousness. This is the observer, as well as the realm of Intuition.

The 3rd consciousness is compassion, stripped away of any perception of separation. This is the source as well as the realm of Emotion. At this level, you experience the root of all physical form as the 1st consciousness dissolves into the illusion that it is and the 2nd consciousness aligns itself with the truth of its source: compassion. To return to the 1st consciousness and align it, too, with its source of compassion creates a unified field. This alignment or lack thereof affects how manner manifests in the physical world. To align oneself with compassion from that depth affects the physical manifestation of matter around you. Let's call this state of alignment Cn^3.

Here is an example. Say you're going through a time of depression. You can't eat. Your emotions feel heavy and overwhelming and you can't seem to muster the energy to pull yourself out of it. Physical reality appears different when you are depressed. Your acute imbalance affects the physical senses, as well as the entire body. Your perception of physical things like trees and cars and water actually takes on a different light. In this state, you do not experience M-Theory, the miracle of life. Intellect is instead bombarding the system with messages defining your lack and illness, filled with judgment. Stories are being told about your past and your worthlessness, fueled by Emotion filled with fear, self-loathing, and helplessness. Not only do you not notice the miracle of that tree, you might not even see the tree at all.

In this state your 1st consciousness is not aligned to the source. This causes interruption in the vital flow of the electromagnetic energy of your domain manifesting as illness, conflict and separation.

When you finally do make a healthy recovery, physical reality looks new and alive. As your mind replaces the messages of lack and judgment with ones of hope and compassion, you begin to notice things you had previously been unaware of. The act of embracing your fear and self-loathing in non-judgment, humor and joy makes room for compassion to live within you. You are so grateful to have regained your balance that you actually see things differently. You can stop and smell the flowers, and look deeply into the tree and appreciate the miracle of its creation. The math used to arrange the molecules to experience life from the depressive state is actually a different formula than when you're aligned with compassion.

ALL YOU NEED IS LOVE

The first step to aligning yourself to compassion at this level is committing your consciousness to this task every day. Make a commitment before you rise in the morning to be as fully awake and aware as possible to this task of alignment. Reminding yourself daily reinforces the intent. Plus, you don't want to miss a thing in this evolution of change.

Before you open your eyes in the morning, take a moment with eyes closed to focus on your 2nd consciousness. Feel the table and the wind blowing; sense the physical world from the space between the molecules. Then breathe in the breath of life. With this focus you bring a simple unity of self that allows you to influence the creation of your world throughout the day. In this state of inward focus you can plant the seeds of your intention. What do you want to create today? Intend them into your imagination from this focused state. Intend yourself upon the physical events and experiences of your world by making the commitment and intention to allow the 3rd consciousness to come forth through you and affect every decision that you make.

By setting your intentions, you impact the co-creation of the world. Let's say, for example, that every day you sought out the space between the molecules of the 2nd consciousness and set an intention to bring peace to as many situations as you find that day. When you open your eyes back to the 1st consciousness, wherever you then encountered conflict, your 2nd consciousness reminds you of your intention. You then have an opportunity to change your focus from what you perceive outside yourself in a conflict to what is happening within yourself and how to use the power of your compassion to make a decision to impact the situation towards a positive, regenerative outcome for the good of the whole.

It's important to remember, though, that if your 1st consciousness, or Intellect, does not subjugate itself to the what Intuition is impelling it to do, you will make decisions based on only the limited perception of Intellect, and not for the good of the whole, thereby contributing to a degenerative outcome. Creating Cn³ is about taming the wild horses of Intellect to carry out the desire of the whole as directed through Intuition. As Emotion (compassion from the source) flows through the prism of Human Intention it takes the first step of separation from the source to create Intuition. Intuition is the observer of both the inner world (from its position on the inner wave) and the outer world (from its position on the boundary of the domain). Intuition knows the truth of the whole much better than Intellect. By the time this dual wave splits into three and creates the ability to perceive matter through Intellect as well as create free will, all Intellect needs to do is be a faithful servant and implement the suggested movement of Intuition.

When you achieve Cn³, making peace becomes knee jerk. It changes from something you decide to do to something you simply are: a unified field of peace. As you strive to create it within, it reflects outward. When you go along in the status quo of your rampaging Intellect, not aware of your own impact upon the situation, you make decisions from a defensive posture, contributing to the illusion of "us vs. them." But when Intellect implements the message of Intuition, it aligns with the truth: you are co-creating your own world with everyone else and you know everyone to be part of the miracle.

You also clearly understand the impact of your own actions on the creation of your own life. Karma is instant. Now, as a living example, when you inject yourself into the middle of a conflict you can have great impact. This is when people change. They become inspired by the truth to change. You could never make them change or tell them they have to. By changing yourself so profoundly to become the peacemaker you become the change that leads the way for their change. You do not have to wait for someone else to come along and lead you. You can and must become the change that you wish to see in the world.

WILD HORSES

Granted, this is a tremendously difficult job to tame the wild horses of your Intellect. Watch while you lie there with your eyes closed focused on the 2nd consciousness. Intellect will be creating stories, which will run in your imagination, as to who is right and who is wrong, or what should have been done, what happened yesterday or what might happen tomorrow, what might take place this afternoon, or any number of other intellectual smokescreens. Put those voices in the shadows with the chair and turn your focus deeper inward to your own source of power. From the place of Witness remove your focus from those stories (thereby preserving precious life energy) and redirect it into the inner self (thereby increasing the power and unity). At this level, so close to the source, the stories of Intellect become a part of the one song of the Universe.

Listen for the tone and touch the truth about your own creation. Take accountability for the decisions your own free will makes, and consciously commit to participate in aligning those decisions with the longing of your compassion. Once aligned in this state of Cn^3, you will have profound and rudimental impact on the world, especially on conflict. If you do this everyday, one step at a time, the impact will be monumental.

Be aware of your voices of culture. Watch the world within you. Observe the conflicts between your Intellect and Intuition and Emotion. Breathe in the truth of the unity.

Let compassion flow up through you, as an understanding of the oneness of all human beings.

Watch the world around you. Each conflict you are engaged in will have its own unique activity. There isn't one pat way to resolve every external conflict, however there is only one road to this kind of alignment: making a commitment to consciously impact external peace by first making peace within.

When coming face to face with the arena of a conflict, step back into the 2nd consciousness and ask, "What might my contribution to this conflict be?" Then get your Intellect out of the way and listen for Intuition to tell you the next most advantageous step. Then, even more importantly, use your free will to take that one step.

What step you are impelled to take in any given conflict will be unique. Sometimes, silence might be called for. Other times, it might be listening to someone who hasn't been heard. Sometimes, it'll mean speaking up. Other times, perhaps you will be impelled to distract or redirect. Each situation will have its unique Intuitive answer based on the unique circumstance of that present moment. Your job is to listen and observe and be committed to act on the Intuitive message of compassion.

If you work at this long enough, Intellect eventually aligns with the truth of the oneness and the timeless miracle of it all. It finally quiets down and understands its role in creation as balance and unity are restored. With energy not being drained into thinking about possible futures, making judgments and regretting what has already transpired, it is relieved not to have to work so hard. All Intellect ever has to do is listen to and honor the impelling messages of Intuition.

Until you can manage Intellect, allow it rant away as you put it in the shadows with the table and the chair and the road and the wind.

BECOME THE CHANGE YOU WISH TO SEE

You have an opportunity to be the visionary. Do not just become a person who understands the concept of Cn^3 intellectually. Be a person who puts those concepts of compassion into action every day. Go deep into the space between the molecules and align with the truth of your own unity and compassion.

The science of compassion isn't just about helping human beings to reach your full potential as creators. It's about bringing harmony and regeneration to the environment, the government, businesses, religion, your own local community, everything. It's about the Universe of the Earth working its way back into life after a period of depression. It's about each individual committing to being committed and accountable for their impact as a way to create heaven on Earth.

Know that you are participating in the evolution of consciousness. Ask, "How can I serve? How can I bring peace to my inner world so I can bring peace in outer world?" Each person who makes such a commitment becomes part of this exponential force moving across this planet like wildfire.

It is our hope that enough individuals can commit to the science of compassion that they can manifest the disappearance of nuclear weapons from the face of the earth. Not because any government bans them, although that would happen. Not because companies quit making them, but that, too, will happen. The only true way to disarm the planet is from the space between the molecules of as many individual human beings possible to consciously commit to compassion on such a deep level that we rearrange all the molecules on Earth from her very root.

Intending your day and your personal commitment for peacemaking is evolution. That is present-moment, "here and now" evolution. However, what happens when you fall out of alignment, no matter how hard you try to intend your day? What do you do when you get triggered and end up jumping right into the conflict fueling the fire and creating hellish karma for yourself? What do you do when Intellect gets control and floods the 1st consciousness with stories and judgments and time lines, while at the same time Emotion is stirring up like a hurricane? Intuition might be telling you the next most advantageous step, but Intellect is having none of it. This is perhaps the most crucial point of decision-making and the most important time to remember your commitment to evolution and your desire to impact the planet with compassion.

My Stated Intention

I have an intention. With this book, I intend to create a revolution in how humans understand their relationship to their own existence and in particular, how conflict is viewed and understood. I intend for this new perspective to be so revolutionary it effects a monumental change across the planet. Because this change is so monumental and involves redirecting the focus inward, let's call it Conflict Revolution.

Just how do you bring unity and alignment to your own domain? What if someone could give you step-by-step instructions? Would you put them to use? How do you answer this question: "Would you rather prove you are right, or create peace and unity?"

Perhaps most importantly, what will it take to get you to pick up your power and change your perspective?

CONFLICT REVOLUTION

How does the evolution of consciousness on these sub-quantum levels translate into the events and experiences of your everyday world? What does that mean for you on a daily basis, for example, while standing in line at the supermarket when the woman in front of you has 15 items in the 10-item express lane and you are late for an important meeting?

Let us begin with an analogy. Let's say you are sitting in a library, imagining how to fly a plane. Think of the library as your Intellect. You've been there for years, reading books, thinking, mapping out pictures on paper and analyzing the concepts of flight. Perhaps you've even set up a library table to represent the cockpit of the plane with instruments drawn on paper spread out in front of you. You read and study, and practice with your little mock plane. You even close your eyes and imagine what it feels like to fly the plane. You're so good at this that you're actually nauseous imagining of changing altitudes. In that library you learn so much about the mechanics and the dynamics of flying that not only can you explain thoroughly how all the steps work, you might be able to teach someone else how to theoretically fly a plane.

All of the years of studying matter and the nature of reality, all of the science that has evolved through the ages is like that library. The evolutionary step you are undertaking right now is like leaving the library and walking out onto the tarmac, getting into a real plane and taking that plane off the ground into the sky all by yourself. That is a different skill-set, wouldn't you agree? Understanding something intellectually, and creating an event using your body are two completely different activities. The first can prepare you for the other but cannot replace it.

This is the evolution of consciousness: getting out of the library (the realm of Intellect), stepping out onto the tarmac, into your witness and experiencing the truth of the wholeness of yourself. Evolution and the Human Intention's allowance for self-awareness make you a witness to the phenomenon of creation at work within you. Your perception influences the creation of matter. It is an integral part of organizing the details of your life. In this way, you are creating your own reality every single minute of every day. If you expand your perception to include more compassion, you will be able to consciously affect how matter organizes around you. Like walking out to that tarmac and getting into the plane, you begin the empirical experience of the true nature of your own holistic reality. Suddenly, from the air, the library becomes a small speck in a much more expansive landscape.

THE EXPRESS LANE

How does this understanding of the quantum levels of self affect the manifestation of matter while you are participating in the everyday events of your life? How does it translate when you are, say, in the supermarket express lane, angry with the person in front of you with too many items? How do you live in the awareness of this activity of the quantum level, at the same time you're experiencing "real life?" What does that expansion of perception look like? Or perhaps more importantly, what does it feel like? As I said, this is getting you out of the library and onto the tarmac. It's taking your body with you into an active participation in a greater perception of truth.

It is actually much easier to understand than you might think. However, let me warn you, implementing the expansion could very well create a monumental, revolutionary change in your life.

START A REVOLUTION

In order to experience this greater awareness while you are standing in line at the supermarket, the first thing to do is to begin to revolve your focus from your outer world to your inner world. To do this, you start by finding the perspective of your Witness. Step back out of Intellect and its stories, stay in touch with a place near your heart, and then observe the entire situation as if you were a reporter for a national newspaper.

Start to take note of every detail of the external scene: The express lane allows for 10 items but the woman ahead of you actually has 15 items, five more than the limit. Touch your emotions: are you irritated? Angry? Frustrated? Make note of what the voices of culture are saying inside your head: that you are going to be late for an important meeting because of her inconsideration. Watch how you equate the emotion with the details of the story that Intellect and imagination create: that your anger is being caused by the fact that this woman has too many items in her cart and this is going to make you late. Watch as Intellect uses imagination to jump ahead an hour and focus on this possible future. At this point you begin to make judgments as Intellect attaches Emotion to these voices of culture.

Keeping your reporter's eye roving around the scene, pay very close attention to the details of the story of why you are so irked. Listen as Intellect holds her accountable for your Emotion. Be aware of how Intellect now determines she is thoughtless and rude. Pay attention to the judgments: are you thinking she is bad, wrong, or inconsiderate for blatantly disobeying the rules of the express lane? And because of this, do you feel justified in taking action against her by way of being rude to her and expressing just how angry you are because she is so inconsiderate? Perhaps you are thinking and feeling all those things while fighting hard to bite your tongue through your irritation.

These judgments and stories are the thoughts of Intellect, the voices of culture that create the message of separation. This is also the moment where you project onto the other person your own thoughts and feelings. The truth is, on a quantum level she is merely a reflection of a part of you rooted in the same source with just a different angle of reflection. She, quite literally, is you.

Remember: any story of Intellect that does not contain the truth of the unity of the miraculous experience of human life is only a partial truth. Any story that does not contain compassion is only part of the whole. By falling into the trap of the messages of separation, you slip into an "us vs. them" mentality that actually in turn promotes conflict and degenerative decision-making.

If you keep your focus on what's outside of you at 180 degrees, you miss the miraculous manifestation occurring at 0 degrees. Remember, the closer to 0 degrees—true north and real compassion—the more you behave like a wave. The closer to 180 degrees, the more "real" and hard you will be, experiencing "ordinary" matter more like a table, the dirt, your car, your body and the woman in the express lane.

PROJECTION

As you stand in line at the super market, revolve your focus on her from 180 degrees outside yourself back upon yourself and you will see the truth of the unity. The power to perceive human life originates within you. Earth has granted you this power and you are subject to the laws and restrictions of living within the agreements of Earth's environments. The condition of your inner psyche is part of the beautiful dance of cooperation between these complex systems that allow all of life to be perceived. If there is conflict first and foremost within your own psyche, you will unknowingly project your anger onto someone or something else, actually becoming part of creating the conflict in the first place. You must stop, step back and watch yourself first and foremost, before spending any time analyzing anyone else.

So how do you train yourself to get your focus off the reflection in the mirror (the woman with 15 items) and turn it back to 0 degrees (to your own compassion)? How could I inspire you to do such daily work? And even if I could inspire you to do this work, what exactly would that work be? How does one begin to change perspective?

As you focus on the woman in front of you with your reporter's eye, ask yourself questions about her life. Who is she? Where is she going? Does she have children? Did her parents love her? Does she know how many items are allowed in the express lane or did she just not pay attention? Expand your thinking about her past your current emotional-intellectual moment. Begin to understand that, from a molecular level, you and she share the same point of origin. She is literally a part of you. Look at her with that empathy and you will open the door to an evolutionary moment.

As you bring your awareness into the truth of your oneness, begin to view her not as a person outside yourself. See her as a part of you. Regard her as a metaphor, an event that has been created outside you as a reflection of something within you.

The idea here is that your decisions create your karma. It does not matter how wrong, inconsiderate or rude she is, if you act rude and inconsiderate by lashing out at her with words or deeds, you are only hurting yourself by creating the math of your own bad karma. In that way, you have absolutely no affect on anyone's karma but your own. At the same time, you are co-creating that moment through your own perspective. Your subjective perception and how you choose to act will have a great impact on what you experience from that situation.

As you stand in that supermarket express lane, notice that the greater the intensity of the emotion projected into her, the more real your perception becomes. Therefore, if Intellect has created a judgmental, hate-filled description of this rude woman being fueled by anger, that description becomes your reality. You are so focused on 180 degrees you aren't aware of the origin of the reflection. Things become very real at that degree. In this case, the chances are great that you will decide to act out against her, as if you are justified by these half-truths of Intellect. That decision instantly becomes part of the math of your karma, sure to come back around into the center of your domain and show up as the next wave to hit you in the back of the head. In this way, you truly are creating your own world.

By stepping back into your Witness and reporting on the bigger picture, you set yourself up to be able to change your relationship to this activity and consciously make different decisions based on the good of the whole. By changing the stories of Intellect, you can change your decisions and therefore your impact upon the situation and your own karma. Understand that the woman in the supermarket line is a member of your family, another human being struggling through life. Choosing to treat her with compassion not only influences her situation for a greater good, but also balances your own karmic math.

THE TRIGGER

Emotion will trigger you to awareness of the need to change the judgmental voices of culture playing inside your head. Being triggered by Emotion is the experience of being twitchy and irked, the "red flag" signaling its time to get out of the Intellect/Library and onto the tarmac, into Witness. Emotion will also trigger the voices of culture, ready with the story that assesses and judges the current situation. When Emotion couples with these voices of culture, realities are born.

Witness is observing Intellect, Intuition, Emotion, Spirit and Itself. Witness is a synergistic reflection of the whole of your parts. As Human Intention separates the oneness into these parts, the Witness brings the parts back together into a unified field of focus. The synergy of all the parts coming together able to understand and experience the entire event for what it truly is brings you back into oneness, back to your true north. Choosing to act in compassion aligns your free will and deeply affects how you influence that woman in the express lane.

But perhaps even more importantly, making conscious choices to act in compassion also changes the Earth's gravity wave. As all humans possess the same math as the Earth and travel on the same gravitational lines, when you bring unity and peace to your part of the wave, you change the Earth as well. Miraculously, mysteriously, you actually change the world beyond the levels of conscious thinking.

BECOME CLARK KENT/SUPERMAN

So how do you watch yourself and what do you see when you watch? And what do you do when you actually witness yourself fueling Emotion into a story that Intellect is projecting onto someone else that then creates a conflict that seems so real?

Changing perception requires self-inspiration. For so long your inner world has been a blur. Stepping into Witness allows you to distinguish between Intellect and Emotion. You have mistakenly thought that all the intellectual energy spent making up stories about why you feel the way you do has been feeling your feelings. You are exhausted, having so many "issues" to deal with so many people, expending your precious energy talking through them. Years of psychotherapy have you hashing through the stories of Intellect over and over again. You imagine this is feeling your feelings. In reality, that is pure intellectual energy that is stopping the flow of Emotion. The true act of feeling

Emotion is an entirely different skill set. Chances are you actually use your over-intellectualizing to not have to feel your feelings. No wonder you get exhausted!

In order to experience the purity of Emotion intimately in present moment, you must step into Witness, detach from those voices of culture and replace them with the voice of Intuition. Intuition will tell you the next most advantageous step to take for the good of the whole situation, regardless what Emotion is flowing through you. Chances are, when you are being triggered by Emotion, Intuition is more than likely impelling you to stop, while Intellect is goading you on to take action against the perceived source of your discomfort. Intellect has final say over what you choose to do, thus has the final say over your own karma. How often does your Intellect actually implement the impelling of Intuition?

This point within human psyche, where Intellects chooses to override the impelling of Intuition, is the root of all conflict that manifests in the world around you. This is where the revolution, therefore the resolution will take place.

So there you stand in line behind this inconsiderate, rude woman who you have now determined is responsible for making you angry. Your stomach is in a knot because you are late; the wild horses of Intellect are trampling through your mind with stories of her evil. You are about to give her a good what for. Instead you hold your tongue until she is gone and then make a disparaging remark to the checkout clerk about her. Can you begin to understand how you are shooting yourself in your own foot?

When you notice your stomach in a knot, or your skin getting twitchy, then hear the judgmental voice of culture focused on something outside you, step into Witness and pay close attention to this event taking place. Listen closely to the voices of culture, judging her, making her responsible for your feelings. As you listen, you will hear a reoccurring theme running through the story. If you listen long enough, you can parboil down the general theme of your story into smaller bits of information.

Is she is rude? Inconsiderate? Is she inconveniencing you? Did she break the rules? Explain it thoroughly. Listen carefully. Articulate clearly what she is "doing to you" and then prepare to turn all those descriptions, judgments, observations and conclusions back to 0 degrees, upon yourself. This is the point of the revolution.

From the place of Witness, begin to examine your own life against those descriptions. Where in your life have you been rude? Where do you break the rules? Where do you inconvenience others?

Much like a hamster on a wheel, Intellect will take you around and around and around, burning up precious energy, creating bad karma all over the place, contributing fuel to the fire of any conflict you are involved in. This cyclic thinking, focused on something outside yourself, is really rooted in this question: If the woman in the supermarket line makes you so mad because she is rude, imagine how you must feel when you are rude. And how in the world can you expect to be the one to hold her responsible for her rudeness when you have no idea the extent of your own?

Yes, Intellect will insist that this is not about you being rude. No, in that moment, perhaps you are not experiencing a direct mirror of your own life. Perhaps your reflection is from years, or lifetimes ago. Here in Afterlife, time slows to a crawl and there is a great deal of space between the molecules. In this state, sometimes time is cloudy, and the reflection you are faced with is from a darker part of your past. Perhaps you made decisions when you had been drinking, or unaware of your life. Even though you made the decision under the influence of alcohol does not mean you still aren't responsible for the karma you created.

Unfortunately (or not) you have no power over the woman in line at the supermarket. You do, however, have self-awareness and free will and can make new decisions about how you yourself will choose to act.

WHERE YOUR POWER LIES

In that supermarket line, instead of focusing on these stories about her, use your time to think about your life. Get your focus off her and begin to remember the times that you might have inconsiderate or rude. Don't allow Intellect to tell you that you are not. Because chances either during your present life or other lifetimes you have lived, somewhere, somehow you made decisions that were rude and inconsiderate to others.

Self-scrutinize from your Witness. Was it just last week when you yourself tried to slip a few extra items into your cart for the express lane and made someone else late? Or did it have absolutely nothing to do with the grocery store? Perhaps you lost your temper with the customer service rep on the telephone and said disparaging things to her. Maybe you yelled at your brother needlessly. Perhaps you were rude to the driver ahead of you going too slow in the passing lane. Did you give them a hand gesture that might have been considered rude?

The point is you go through life unconscious of the consequences of these simple acts. Conflict Revolution brings home to roost where your power really lies on an intricate, intimate level.

Sometimes when you are emotionally triggered by something as horrific as war or murder, acts that you know you did not commit in this life, remember that your consciousness has been part of creating the Earth since the beginning of its inception. You have had many lives through the ages, some more than likely involved participating in war, or could have been lived as a murderer. You must commit to the mystery so as not to allow your Intellect to convince you that you ("us") are more innocent than her ("them").

Each time Intellect defines Emotion as sourced in something outside yourself, you lose touch with the inner Emotion. The part of the gravitational wave that is Emotion, which is monitoring the condition of the whole, stops flowing outward and literally becomes trapped in your physical body. Here, if trapped long enough, it can create physical and mental illness, as well as conflicts in the outer world.

If you do have the wherewithal to actually remember a time when you chose to act rudely just like the woman ahead of you in the line, you will also find the trapped Emotion created by that choice that you are now erroneously sourcing outside you. Revolving your perspective, you now can touch the inner wave of Emotion generated by your decision to be rude to someone else. Even if you can't remember a specific act of rudeness, commit to the mystery of this revolutionary new perspective and admit that you very well could have, at some time in your life, acted as this woman is right now.

FEELING AND BREATHING

In this way you can begin to align Intellect with messages that support looking inward and feeling and breathing. This will begin to release the trapped Emotion and get it flowing through you again.

You don't need to know *why* you feel any emotion, you just need to *feel* it. You don't need to project this emotion onto the woman in front of you, just take a deep breath, feel your feeling and then release it. Just stand there and breathe Emotion deep into your body. Think of Lamaze breathing. When you are having a baby there is no stopping those labor pains. Feeling Emotion is not something you control. It's meant to flow through you like electromagnetic energy, without judgment, without stories, without projection onto the woman in the express lane. You don't get up and decide to do a little happiness around noon and work in a little fear and grief later on in the afternoon. Just standing there in the supermarket line you are going to be feeling Emotion as a function of experiencing this precious human life. You will not always know where it came from or what its about. All you need to do to feel and release it is to get your focus off the stories of Intellect and breathe while you feel. Feeling and breathing the electromagnetic energy of Emotion, you can now own every last compilation of it as your own.

While you cannot "control" the flow of electromagnetic waves of Emotion, what you do need to control are your actions around how you choose to articulate those feelings. Choosing to lash out at someone outside yourself as the source of your Emotion is like slapping your own face. There is no need to lash out or blame anyone when you understand how Emotion truly works in the bigger picture of the whole of the psyche. No one ever taught you this before. Evolving humanity has never been to this point of consciousness.

The truth is that you may not know exactly what decision you made along the way to be rude or inconsiderate like the woman ahead of you in the supermarket line. Every rude and inconsiderate action you took created the math of your gravity that has been circulating through you. Each time you focused outside yourself and passed off your Emotion as being caused by someone else, you unwittingly prevented the emotional part of that wave from fully flowing through you. Emotion then became trapped in your physical body. That anger rising in the supermarket line could be part of a trapped emotion generated 20 years ago when you were rude and considerate to someone else that has nothing whatsoever to do with the woman in front of you.

FEEL AND BREATHE

How often in a day do you take time to feel and breathe Emotion? This is a vital step to reconnecting the parts of the inner psyche. When you allow waves of Emotion to flow through you without judgment, attachment or actions taken against someone, they continue outward to the edge of your domain where they are swept back to realign with true north of Earth and start again from the core. Only this time, instead of containing math of lashing out or trying to hurt someone, they re-enter your being the math of compassionate resulting of actions taken in love, wholeness and non-judgment. The truth becomes what you are, not just what you think. You have stepped out of the library and are in flight, participating with your entire being, not just your imagination.

So step into the witness and watch Intellect run on like wild horses stampeding through your brain creating stories and judgments, fueling them with fear and anger and projecting them on other people. You do the same with stories about saviors and soul mates and healers fueled by desperation and isolation. Begin to consider that the part of your spiritual body known as Emotion exists independently of those stories. You can have a relationship to Emotion that is independent of Intellect. You can actually become your fear, pain, anger, as well as all your love and joy as electromagnetic energy moving through you without having an intellectual story that then focuses on something outside of your domain.

FREE WILL

Conversely, you can have a relationship to Intellect independent of Emotion. Intellect has a specific purpose and a different math than Emotion, and is the realm of free will. To expect Intellect to feel Emotion would be like asking your stomach to pump blood and your heart to digest food. Both have function and purpose in the balance of the whole but cannot do each other's job. Intellect was never meant to feel Emotion. It was meant to implement the command of Intuition that supports Emotion flowing through you freely, without blame, shame or attachment.

As you watch, you will begin to see Intellect creating judgments and stories that then get anchored with Emotion in your imagination. You'll be able to watch Intellect hijack the whole and make a decision based on a lie. Intuition can be telling you to turn left, and Intellect can decide to go straight without even batting an eye.

It will be astounding as you watch all this functioning and wonder, "Who knew?" You will begin to realize you have been living inside the library of Intellect, in that huge imagination, which is an entirely different perspective than stepping out on the tarmac and watching yourself function in real time.

WHAT DO YOU WANT TO CREATE?

But what is the point of this change of perspective? What happens when you change your life to live more aligned with your true nature, not aligned to the stories and judgments that Intellect tells you?

When you honor Emotion with this compassionate attention, you engage in the decision to practice self-love. Not self-aggrandizing or self-promotion. Self-love is taking care to fulfill your own emotional needs. You only ever have one emotional need: to feel and breathe them all as they come through you. Period. You don't need to hash through the "issues" because there are no issues, only the voices of culture trying to convince you of a partial truth and distract you from the act of feeling and breathing.

Detach from those voices of culture and breathe in the present-moment passion of whatever feeling is coming through you. You don't need to know why, how or what you feel. It is not bad or good, it simply is. You only need to feel it. This is taking care of your own emotional need and getting the flow moving through you. No one else on the planet can do it for you. No one makes you feel a certain way and no one can feel your feelings for you.

This act of self-love changes everything. It quiets and aligns Intellect with Intuition telling you the next most advantageous step. Because you are now taking care of your own emotional need, you no longer seek outside yourself for that person, place or thing to fulfill you or to blame for the conflict. Now you are free to sit back and just feel and breathe Emotion, listen to Intuition and be committed to use Intellect to do its bidding.

Does the small voice telling you the next most advantageous step say, "Stop and rest?" What will it take to get you to actually do it? Watch as Intellect argues all the reasons why you shouldn't, can't and won't rest. Listen as Intellect gets louder and louder, drowning out that still small voice until it bullies you into doing anything but the one step that would be best for the whole. Then you end up burning a candle at both ends, falling ill, starting fights or out of sorts.

Ask yourself: what do you want to create? Do you really want to contribute to the conflict of the Earth by maintaining a defense of separation? Wars are fought as if to "protect" countries and freedom. What if unknowingly that attitude is actually destroying you? What if the only thing that can protect you is your good karma in the end?

Through the ages patriotism has fueled conflicts by promoting "us vs. them" and demeaning those who choose the way of nonviolence. Why is it any more patriotic to die as a soldier committing the act of killing than it is to die in a statement of nonviolent resistance? This is why it is so difficult to weed out the bad decision making: sending youth to fight for patriotism only reinstates the killing karma back into Earth. If those young people marched off to use nonviolence to face what appears to be evil, they may not survive (as they likely wouldn't in convention war) but they would not be adding bad karma back into Earth and onto their own souls by becoming killers themselves.

This cycle of bad karma makes it appear that war is just a part of human functioning. Nothing could be further from the truth.

Human beings at this time have the opportunity to make an evolutionary step. So what do you want to mold yourself into? What do you want to create? Let me make a suggestion.

Consider committing to the work of molding Intellect into a spiritual organ that reflects the truth of compassion (unity), as opposed to reflecting the voices of culture (separation). By stepping into Witness, you can observe the workings of Intellect and slowly change your thoughts to those more aligned to the true nature of your origins of compassion. In this way you actually change Human Intention. When you work to retain nonjudgmental and compassionate thoughts that support feeling and breathing present-moment Emotion and acting on Intuition, you align this organ of Intellect with the mysterious source of compassion springing from the nothingness of the Void.

By changing your relationship to Intellect and Emotion, you affect the condition of the Human Intention that affects the entire planet. Like removing cataracts to improve the opacity of the lens of the eye, changing the condition of the Human Intention at the root allows others to experience that change as well. By changing the condition of the Human Intention, you become Cn^3, the change you wish to see in the world.

BACK IN THE SUPERMARKET LINE
So there you are with this woman, rude and inconsiderate. Remember that whatever you perceive outside of yourself is a reflection of your inner world. How much are your voices of culture influencing your decision-making? What will you decide to say to her, and why? These are the questions that must be asked in this intricate moment that only you can ask of yourself.

If you revolve your conflict and examine your own life while you feel and breathe Emotion, you begin to experience your anger in a new way. When the anger arises, you reach for the message of compassion, already in place, that says, "I don't need to know what these emotions are about, I just need to feel them. Just breathe…breathe…breathing is always part of feeling… feeling and breathing." Get Intellect's focus off of the woman ahead of you in line and onto feeling and breathing instead. It's not that your mind will necessarily instantly become calm. Witness might still watch Intellect rant on and on about the injustice of those five extra items. But the operative point is what decisions are you going to make about Emotion and Intellect, and how will those decisions impact your world?

As you listen to your voices of culture define her, look at her more like you might interpret a dream. If you had dreamt about her, some dream analysts might say she represents a side of you. With this in mind, revolve your perspective. Begin to ask yourself, how are you like her? Where are your disrespectful thoughts? What is your emotion around them? When are you rude? When do you break the rules and inconvenience other? Because when you watch yourself, you catch yourself in the act of making choices to be against someone. You find out how cruel you can be.

Witness also discovers Emotion within: fear, shame, depression, even hate. This is when you need to commit to develop a new way to release your feelings without projecting them on the woman in line at the supermarket, or your husband or children or neighbor or friends or strangers on the street.

You need a regime for caring and nurturing Emotion as it flows through you. Like childbirth, your feelings will rise up in their own time and space. In that moment, all you ever need to do is align Intellect with compassionate thoughts and feel and breathe, being conscious of Emotion moving through your body.

"COME, PASSION!"

Compassion can be infused into your relationship to all your emotions. Can you have compassion for your anger? Of course you can. You can be steaming mad without having a story or judgments as to why you are so. Intellect can be celebrating this anger coming through you, saying, "Thank God I have the power to feel all my emotions and release them instead of projecting them onto others!" while you stand in the supermarket line feeling and breathing. No one even has to know you are mad. This change in your relationship to your anger makes your energy less destructive and influences on unseen levels the decision you make in that supermarket line.

Who knew that standing in line at the supermarket could be an opportunity to heal your Human Intention and forever change the way you experience yourself and the world? Once you experience yourself choosing to be disrespectful of this miraculous experience of life, regardless of what Intellect has been telling you to justify your actions, you can no longer deny the impact you have upon the manifestation of matter.

By consciously embracing the shame, fear or anger while choosing to align Intellect with non-judgment and compassion, you have now chosen to actively participate in creation by exerting the science of compassion. This reorganization of how your Human Intention is manifesting gravely affects how the particles will organize into matter. It also heals forever your portion of the Human Intention. You change matter at the root. One person at a time, this is eventually how you will rid the world of war and violence.

FORGIVE FORGIVE FORGIVE

If you can forgive yourself for being a disrespectful idiot, humbly loving yourself, what do you see when you then turn your focus back to the woman in line? How much different does she look? Now that you've explored the root of your conflict and resolved it there, how will you respond to her?

If you are no longer attached to the reflection of her, but indeed have refocused on compassion and taking accountability for your own rude decisions, you may not care that she has those extra items. She may appear more human to you. You feel empathy for her because she is indeed a part of you. And now she has taught you a valuable lesson of empowerment and she doesn't even know it! You might feel downright generous with her and help her get her bags to her car.

In the end, now you know: all life dissolves back into the Void again. The rest is projection and mystery. I can tell you from experience that when you die, all you take with you is the karma of the decisions that you made in life and what you are emotionally and intellectually attached to. If on your death bed you are angrily attached to some illusion that the voices of culture tell you, you will bring that relationship between Intellect and Emotion with you, embedding its math in the Human Intention only to be recreated again the next time your consciousness emerges to create human life.

This is what happened to me. As my senses were fading on my deathbed, I could not detach from the horror of the idea that I helped create the potential destruction of all human life. That burden has followed me into Afterlife. Because of that attachment, I have dedicated all my consciousness to bringing about illumination to help heal human hearts so they will not use the weapons of mass destruction that inhabit Earth today.

Don't stop asking yourself: What do you want to create with your priceless life energy? Do you want to be right or do you want to make peace? I am not just implying world peace on some nebulous level. What do you want to make of your own life?

Only you have the answers.

Science & Religion

Humanity is headed in a direction where all parts of the whole must not only understand the need to learn to work together, but then by working together get to know the other parts in such a way that brings the reality of unity into a bodily experience.

Now is the time for everyone to realize that they are but a piece to a bigger puzzle that is mysterious by nature. Science and religion are only two pieces to that puzzle. The differences of science and religion don't need to become divisive. Differences are not causing the derision. Even similarity can cause division. When you see something in someone else that mirrors a part of you that you truly hate, those similarities do not in and of themselves foster unity. What brings unity is the change in perception from separate beings to one being, which will change consciousness.

Perception must change from being myopically focused on one part of the whole as the only part of the whole. Science cannot claim that they are the whole, although they have an important part of it. Religion cannot claim to be the whole, but they have another important part. Commerce, corporations, business, politics, moneymaking, none can claim to be the whole, but they are an important part of it. Even feeding the hungry and housing the homeless cannot be all that there is, but it is certainly an important part of the whole.

I am not saying don't house the homeless and feed the hungry. But a society completely focused on only providing shelters for the homeless creates a dependency on that activity. Just as a society only focused on war as a solution to conflict will manifest matter into the event of war, only because matter manifests on what Human Intention is focused. You must focus on understanding the root causes of homelessness and war and transforming your perception of them by aligning with compassion. As a society, you must learn to create instead of destroy, learn the power that you yourselves hold in your physical matter. You will either all learn to get along, or you will destroy life as you know it.

So you see, science and religion are dependent upon each other for their survival and the evolution of the planet. And this is what you've come to, the question of survival of the species.

This is a critical moment in evolution. We must wed ethics with science, because science is a key element in spawning the biggest weapons of war. That does not make science inherently evil. It means that humans in positions of power who remain conflicted on a root level will continue to mistakenly project that inner conflict onto the world around them and use those weapons of war to manifest chaos and destruction.

Religion must learn to go deeper to the root of its own meaning. All the beautiful and inspiring stories of holy men do not mean that those holy men were any more inherently divine than you. It means that humans who remain attached to their subjective interpretation of the dogma of their teachings will seek outside themselves for their source to actually become the evil they so fear and unknowingly contribute to the separation and ultimately the demise of this planet.

Evolution and survival of the species require reprogramming Human Intention to align with compassion, the act of tuning up and into the one song of the universe. Religion must teach people how to access and use their own power from their source within, in the spirit of the great teachers. No longer can any one religion use the argument that they are the "right" and "only" religion to the exclusion of others. Recognize that this perception creates conflict at a root level by excluding the truth of the whole. Every religion is the "right" religion, because it is not religion in and of itself that is divine. It is human beings using the precepts of spiritual teachings as a pathway to the source within that brings the spirit of all religions to life.

Such a grand experiment this is! No humans who came before you had to grapple with this as a part of ultimate survival. But then again, never before has the world been so armed and dangerous. Never before has humankind been at the brink of possible self-annihilation as they are today.

This change to regenerative manifestation is achieved through detachment from the illusion of the 1st consciousness. These are the steps to evolutionary survival and you who are willing to take the journey inward and expand your everyday, waking consciousness to commit to the science of compassion are the missing link.

Remember, no matter what happens to your planet, the galaxies will live on. If Earth blows itself up, the affect upon the totality of the universe as you presently know it will be imperceptible to a great deal of the cosmos. So what seems like the huge and utter devastation of an entire species and a planet will have a small affect on the whole.

This does not mean that human life is not sacred. You should be doing everything in your power to eliminate the possibility of self-annihilation. But if that scenario does play out, the need to inflict pain and suffering on other people in the name of what is right will be dwarfed by the truth of the effect upon the planet. The need to prove you are right will ultimately be what destroys you. Yet Earth's demise would make barely a ripple in the fabric of the cosmos of billions of galaxies. The energy of the universe continues, and your consciousness returns to the Void only to again become a part of the compassionate urge to create human life.

However, if you manage to destroy your precious home Earth, your consciousness will bring with it the programming to recreate the entire event in the next creation. Though it might take billions of years, consciousness will repeat this process of creation and destruction until enough conscious souls have attained a level of awareness that sees through the illusions of degeneration and war and makes the conscious choice to act in compassion. This will then be the creation of the ultimate physical manifestation of heaven, heaven literally being the planet that births you.

In the search for other intelligence in the cosmos, scientists have not uncovered anything like humans. That doesn't mean that there is no other life in the cosmos. Contrary, the cosmos is teeming with life and consciousness. There is indeed a very intelligent design, one rooted in mystery and the eternity of the circle of the strings, playing the one song. From my seat, there is no doubt about this. However, because our species is born from and aligned to the electromagnetic energy field of Earth, life in other parts of the galaxy will look differently than us mere humans, as their consciousness is aligned to the electromagnetic forces of the planet from which they are born.

You Are The Instrument

The challenge for science is that they believe that the tools they need to measure this quantum level of consciousness have not been created yet. They think because they cannot see with instruments past 10^{-35} that they cannot study consciousness yet. Yes, there will be instruments in the future to measure the consciousness of the unified fields in a way that you cannot today.

However, the ultimate instrument available to you right now is your own living consciousness: Intellect, Emotion, Intuition, Witness, Spirit, your physical body, your membrane domain. Inspire and commit yourself to studying and observing these elements within yourself every day to instigate and measure the expansion of your own consciousness. Experiment over and over with your perception and study the resulting manifestation of matter. In the true spirit of advancing science, become the experiment. Like Faraday, who sent electric current through live wires and watched the affect on magnets, study how channeling your energy into different thoughts, emotions and ultimate actions affects the world around you. Watch how your interpersonal relationships with the other humans reflect the true nature of the condition of your own Human Intention. Entertain these suggested perceptions not as truth or because they are the "right" perceptions. Play with this self-change of perspective as a scientist might. Only don't just be willing to be proven wrong. Be also willing to be proven right.

This practice of taking responsibility for the true nature of your own power can be applied to religion as well. Remember: heed the lesson, not the teacher. The message is that God creates everything, even evil. The only evil you have control over is that which originates in you. Directing energy towards someone else as the source of your evil without first looking at your own impact on the situation is itself evil. Clinging to your religion as the "right" one for all, casting judgments on "them" without also scrutinizing yourself, and forcing this perception onto others is the evil to be addressed in modern religion. This is making decisions for the good of the part over the good of the whole. This then creates the separation that, if left unchecked, will manifest as your fabled war of the end of the world.

If you yourself are inadvertently fostering separation, you will not burn in hell because someone wrote it in a book and claimed it would be so. It would also not be because your holy man insists it to be so and you must believe your holy man. You burn in hell as the direct result of cause and effect of your own decisions. All your actions in life that foster separation also feed the suffering you experience after the death of your physical body as hell. Fostering separation is living a lie. The truth of the unity of matter on a quantum level of consciousness negates the power of the illusion of separation. From this perspective you will find the power to transform your own injurious nature at the root. Catch evil at this level and you will change the entire outcome of evolution.

This does not mean that there are not others outside you who perform evil acts. It only means that you can only control what is within your own domain. To seek outside yourself to destroy what you see in the mirror of other people creates your own bad karma.

Remove the judgment of "evil" for a moment in an attempt to understand it. Separation is a necessary part of being able to experience life as a human being. Human Intention separates the gravitation waves emanating from the Void in order to bring sound, color and light into focus. It's when Intellect uses free will to act for the sake of the part over the welfare of the whole that degenerative processes develop. But see how Intellect creates horrible stories of suffering and destruction around this word "evil" that are then fueled by fear and blame of the evil of someone or something outside you. Remove the judgment and understand evil to be the illusion of separation that begins within. Don't allow Intellect to hold you hostage to subjective meanings and unattended emotions.

To fight something "evil" outside you with destructive actions only sucks you into becoming evil yourself. There is no regeneration when humans murder each other for the sake of being "safe."

SCIENCE AND RELIGION: INTELLECT AND EMOTION

Science and religion simply must accept that they need each other. They are the Intellect and Emotion of human society. Each inspires in unique ways, and like the heart and the kidneys, each have a special function only they can fulfill. Their root of Human Intention is the same, but their output is different.

However, if they are both committed to making peace instead of being right, they would powerfully influence evolution. The product of one body, these two organs have so much in common. Science can easily say, "We are all one; this is a mystery that cannot be solved," then keep looking deeper to solve it. Religion can easily say, "We are all one; this is a mystery that cannot be solved," then live deeply in the faith of its truth. What difference does it make, as long as each is willing to accept the mystery?

Divergence merely reveals the unique purpose to each: Asking "what?" science as Intellect proceeds to a deeper, empirical understanding of that mystery from a quantum level; asking "how?" religion as Emotion goes on to inspire the hearts and the minds of humans to continually align to compassion. There are just as many interpretations of religion as there are of science. Either is merely information filtered through the hearts and the minds of the individuals who are the scientists, who are the religious, who are the people seeking to expand their consciousness. Science and religion are only as good as the people who practice them.

EVOLUTIONAL CREATIONISM

This change you are being asked to make is not a spiritual pursuit, although you use spiritual energy to make it. This is not based in faith, nor is it just imagination. This change is an empirical, scientific self-study, rooted in mystery, done by consciously participating in observation of self. It is indeed an evolutionary study of quantum creation.

The only way we will save the world is by transforming human nature through the cooperative efforts of Intellect and Emotion so that Intuition can be the guiding force for the voice of compassion. It is through the transformation of each individual human heart that the world will evolve. Let go of your focus on the hard objects, step back in your Witness and take care of your inner life. Working for change from there will actually prevent conflict before it begins. In this way you create your own world.

BECOME A RELIGIOUS SCIENTIST

This marriage of science and religion living through you will evolve the planet. Your own belief system coupled with your own empirical experiences should meet in the middle, in the realization of the cause and effect of your own decisions and actions on you and the world around you. As a scientist you should study your own life religiously. As a spiritual being, you should commit to the mystery and accept that no one has a corner on the "right" religion. It is your job to learn to get along with all religions, races, creeds, neighbors, family and yourself.

Subject your experiences to scrutiny, not just of other scientists and holy men but a brutal, compassion and humorous self-scrutiny on a daily, hourly, and quantum basis. Scrutinize the elements of your personal unified field, the focus of your Human Intention that is your domain. This is in essence where all your power lies.

The result of realigning the elements of your unified field to Cn^3 can be thoroughly and rigorously examined. You will see the reflection of this alignment instantly in the world around you. But more than that, merely observing will begin to change the actual condition of your Human Intention. Observation from Witness is the first step that will allow the alignment to true north to take place. In the truth of unity, Intellect will no longer tell stories about the need to be right. You will no longer manifest the lie of separation. Fear may still pass through you, but you will have a new relationship to it. You will teach yourself to feel Emotion. To breathe it in with compassion and acceptance and not allow it to fuel those old lies about someone or something outside yourself as its source. This in turn prevents you from making decisions to take action against someone or something, to think you have to harm someone else to keep yourself safe. In the bigger picture, the only one you need to be safe from is yourself.

No More War

This is how we will eliminate war, one person at a time, starting with you. Each time you choose to have this new, revolutionary perspective, and stand up to take accountability for your own domain, you are changing the gravity of your consciousness and aligning it to true compassion. Because your personal human intention is a part of the bigger wave of Human Intention, all it takes is one person with such a deep and inner intention to start the movement to make a quantum shift. You have the power to reprogram the mechanism on such a deep level, allowing the effects to be far-reaching.

War is an obsolete form of conflict resolution. Holy wars are evil. Nuclear weapons have literally rewritten the math of conflict: there will be no winners in the next world war.

World Peace

Because of this, there is a great movement afoot in your culture right now for peace. People must understand that these problems cannot be solved at the same level at which they were created. This effort to find a new way to deal with conflict is monumental. It's crucial for all who seek peace to commit to be "first from within, then so without." It's crucial to work at peace daily, whether at your workplace, with your family, or in the supermarket line. Every day provides a learning experience on how to choose compassion.

You won't get kudos for this intimate, intricate work. You will be subtly slipping this new perspective into culture while no one is looking. Everyone will be yelling, "Look at that war over there! It's the fault of the a) terrorists, b) president c) culture." But you'll be over here just slowly changing the molecular nature of things from the inside out.

That's what's happening right now. Millions of people on the planet like you are changing the molecular level of their own domain. But all you see or hear on TV, in magazines and newspaper, in all the voices of culture is about the fear, the war, the separation and the conflict. Understand that you as a peacemaker are part of a much bigger network the extent of which you will never see.

Actively participating in Conflict Revolution will indeed create a monumental change for the planet. The excitement is building in Afterlife as we watch the seeds of our intention borne throughout your culture as this book. I always believed that imagination was more important than knowledge, but having this knowledge at this time in your world will hopefully spark your imagination to dream about all that you can possibly achieve if you so choose.

Let yourself dream as big as you can. What do you want to create? Peace with your mother? A steady flow of revenue? Health in your body? No more war? It all begins inside you. Quite literally.

As you proceed to make a revolutionary change in the way you understand your relationship to yourself and thus the world, take time to imagine what you want to create. Listen to Intuition each day. Let it lead you to the next most advantageous step. Watch as you release Emotion trapped for lifetimes now flowing up and out through you by feeling and breathing with compassion. Observe how your Intellect and the voices of culture are now molded around messages of compassion and are doing the bidding of Intuition. See how much less energy you are expending on working through "issues" with everyone and more energy on self-scrutinizing, self-loving and creating.

This conscious effort will change your life forever.

COMPASSIONATE INFRASTRUCTURE

When you align with the voice of Intuition, you change the infrastructure of your own domain that then becomes the reflection in the outer world. That is when the infrastructures of your outer world change as well. Imagine governments, corporations and education built on compassion, with peace as their cornerstone. Imagine a world where your children will come home from school and say, "Daddy I heard that once people killed each other to settle arguments. Is that true?" Imagine that war will be foreign to the children of tomorrow. It may not be soon enough for you to see in this lifetime, but that should not stop you from working towards this ever-important goal.

If there is anything I can do to inspire you to experiment with these new intimate, intricate perspectives, I will do it. Think outside the box and talk amongst yourself to generate new ideas. Talk to your friends, talk to your neighbors and your family, talk to God, Mother Mary, or Albert Einstein. If you need help, ask. Ask and you shall receive. Then, as you commit to this new perspective, watch for small changes in your life. They might be subtle at first, so be aware. Watch carefully. Watch as you change your thoughts and the world manifests differently around you. Watch as you feel and breathe and uncover your heart's desire. Watch and listen for Intuition and use it to guide you on a daily basis. And after all of that, you only need to watch and be amazed.

HEAVEN ON EARTH

Heaven on Earth begins when Intellect finally understands its part in the whole, quiets down and clears room for Intuition to speak and finally be heard. But more importantly Intellect then does the bidding of Intuition, merely following orders derived of the present-moment condition of both the inner and outer world, guided by the source, compassion. Intellect retrains itself to assess the world using only regenerative definitions of oneness, and is committed to simply carrying out what Intuition is impelling it to do. This in turn allows Emotion to flow freely, unblocking lifetimes of pent up energy.

When you choose to tune into the messages of unity, compassion and nonjudgment while allowing yourself to feel and breathe Emotion, the dark energy of Spirit clusters around this new math, affecting the gravity of the ordinary matter of your life. Now your decisions support the integration process. Intellect, which had previously been living in the lie of separation, is now broadcasting messages of truth that are aiding you in experiencing Emotion in a present moment, compassionate way. This eliminates the need to act out onto someone else the fear you feel. Knowing that "they" are not the root of the fear, you can make new choices to not act against, but to act to bring together.

Then watch how ordinary events manifest differently around you. Make note of the changes. Some things will be blatant: a once-cranky neighbor extending herself in kindness; the resolution of a long-standing conflict in your family; an unexpected job offer; healing a physical ailment. Other manifestations might be subtler: life becomes less hectic for a moment; a stressful situation subsides; breathing room appears; you suddenly find hope. Eventually, I believe you will find a definitive connection between aligning Human Intention with compassion, and the peace that manifests in personal as well as global life.

With Human Intention aligned to compassion and the desire to make peace replacing the need to be right, you resolve conflict on the root level thereby eliminating the need to create weapons. You don't have to hurt and destroy others because they are not the source of your conflict. Applying the goal of self-love, the by-product becomes the eventual disarmament of the planet.

It all begins in the heart and mind of ordinary human beings. It begins with you creating a unified field between the personal heart and the personal mind, consequently changing your relationship to the world around you. At any time, any human being can stop and ask his or herself, "Who am I? What impact am I having on this planet? On this situation?" Even if you are blind, deaf and dumb, you can still ask yourself who you are and what impact your decisions are having on the manifestation of your life.

When you are involved in a conflict, ask yourself these questions: Am I standing in my rightness and holding my individual banner as if I am the only one who is right? Am I parading my own self-righteousness in the face of my neighbor, who is under a different banner, a different nationality, a different political party, religion, color-skin, gender? Are they, too, holding their rightness as a fist and making that their priority as well? And what impact are my actions having upon the outcome of the conflict?

Ask yourself, do you need to prove you are right, to set out to destroy something outside yourself as a way to feel safe, or can you stop and consider a new way? Ask yourself, what if you chose to be the one to make the peace, at all costs? Ask yourself: If you are so willing to give up your life fighting in a war that kills other people, would you be willing to give up your life not killing other humans? Ask yourself why does one way to die for freedom negate the other? How do you have a non-violent movement in a nuclear age?

From a quantum level, none of your differences exist. From the source, everything is just potential. There is an innocent future in the Void, where everything and nothing exist as once. Your differences are merely Intellectual voices of culture, fueled by the Emotion of fear, inciting you to make decisions that cause the molecules in the Void to arrange as conflict, dissidence, war. See from a quantum level and you lose the divisiveness and gain the undeniable, empirical experience that you all spring from the same source. You bear witness that you are all essentially one body.

Every human must ask: Do I want to be right or do I want to make peace? These are two different skill sets with two different outcomes. Be warned though! You will find many, many people, yourself included, who at some time will want to be right and will continue projecting their inner conflict onto the world, attaching blame to someone across the street with a different banner.

THIS IS NOT ANTI-WAR

You inadvertently create an "Us vs. Them" mentality when you participate in the anti-war movement. Do not spend time trying to convince those who insist on being right that they are wrong to not want to make peace. You only create the same judgmental condition of separation you so wish to prevent. But more importantly, it insidiously distracts you from and deludes your own power. Those fighting to be right, including you, must find the change within to make peace.

More effective will be finding the peacemakers and instilling in them the importance of resolving their internal conflicts so as not to project them onto the wave of the Void in such a way that contributes to the demise of your world. Those who are willing to listen and learn together, even a minority, could change the fate of the entire human species.

From the perspective of Afterlife, six billion humans, all facets of the same source, are standing side by side on a precipice faced with the fact that deadly arms are embedded all across the planet. Earth is the definitive suicide bomber right now, rigged to blow. What if every single weapon that exists on the planet in 2007 went off at once? You would have a supernova. From this perspective, what would it hurt to ask yourself, "How might I be unknowingly contributing to this situation? What can I do to change myself to have a more positive, powerful, regenerative impact? How can I bring your right and my right together to build an even bigger right?"

MORE THAN YOU KNOW

You have no idea how many humans inhabiting this planet are consciously working for peace. As I said, this has been one of my greatest achievements from Afterlife: inspiring people to work for peace. Millions of them are rallying in the streets, writing to their congress people, meditating and praying in churches, synagogues, temples, mosques, and ashrams. From the mountain tops, mothers and fathers are shouting, "No more war! War is an obsolete form of conflict resolution!" Those people when inspired to individually make peace on this quantum level within can change so much.

In this way, any individual can undertake the job of everyday peacemaking, even if you never go to a peace rally or say a prayer. If every human were committed to this kind of self-scrutiny to find peace on a daily basis from this quantum level, you would evolve the planet. The exponential energy of those actions in a minority of humans could change the consciousness of the entire planet. We the peacemakers must become the change we want to see and let our example lead the way and influence the situation from a quantum level.

People like you, willing to scrutinize yourself daily, are the visionaries of this evolutionary step. The direction of this change has no road map. There aren't instruments to measure it. All you have is your inner gravity and compassion, aligning you to what is true. The rest is your creation. You become everyday visionaries quietly leading the way to the expansion of perception, becoming the instruments to measure consciousness and its affect on the manifestation of matter.

When you become the change, you can then change the institutions of science, religion, politics, and social services, one person at a time starting with you, to support this kind of self-scrutiny. Even within the peace movement, people are reluctant to stop and self-scrutinize at this quantum level. They believe if they fight the war makers they can create peace. But this is not so. Then again, no one has taught you how to truly go within and make peace there first. Perhaps this small volume can be a jumping off point.

WHAT WILL IT TAKE TO GET YOU TO STAND UP?

Who will take this evolutionary step? You have been given a conscious mind that makes the decisions of where and how your energy is expended. Nurturing compassionate awareness of Intellect and its relationship to the whole will alter the direction of this planet towards regeneration and into disarmament.

It won't happen just by changing politics, although it's good to work for political change. It's not about just changing religion or science, but certainly changes must be made there as well. None of those parts of the whole can save the world. What will save the world will be the parts coming together to accept and embrace a new definition of the whole. When enough individual humans begin to ask how to create peace instead of how to prove they're right, then will the world shift on the quantum level.

Being committed to observing the consciousness of your consciousness throughout the day is not about sitting on some mountaintop, away from all the cares of the world with beautiful scenery and nothing to do but meditate. That is not the experience you'll likely have. Change on this level is not easy. Sustaining intimate, intricate self-awareness on a daily basis is one of the hardest things a person can do, especially when you feel the anger, frustration, or helplessness cementing your stories into reality. This imbalance between Intellect and Emotion can grip humans tightly and make them want to lash out and hurt someone else.

Persistence and hard work in your commitment to your own transformation eventually changes the mathematics of your gravity. Once you've changed on this level, choosing compassion becomes as knee-jerk as perceiving separation had been. Now when Emotion rises, an entirely new set of actions kick in, causing new reactions. Intellect knows to empty itself to protect the world from its projections. It tunes into the messages of compassion and uses them to support feeling and breathing Emotion. With nonjudgmental messages of truth and unity from Intuition inspiring you to feel and breathe, you are reminded that, as you breathe in Emotion and embrace it, it becomes a part of your unity. Now you are a living unified field. You are living truth, accepting your power, committed to and capable of contributing to world peace like never before.

If you want to be physically healthy, you create a routine of healthy eating and exercise. If you want to be spiritual, you routinely meditate and pray. If you want to be in politics, you routinely devote time to political causes. So if you want to resolve the conflicts from within, on a routine basis you take time to self-scrutinize.

If you can't get Intellect under control, then step into Witness and listen for clues to your own road map. Ask yourself to define what you think is the cause of your conflict. Then set about to witness where you might be perpetuating these very conditions. Think outside the box.

This kind of accountability and consciousness of the consciousness is beyond science and religion. It is beyond politics and business, beyond humanitarian efforts. It is a transformation of an individual compilation of consciousness on a molecular level, using free will to integrate those parts into the whole to create Cn^3.

This is heaven on earth. And that, dear friends, is the next frontier.

So what will it take to get you to stand up?

Barbara With is an author, composer, performer, psychic, workshop facilitator and inspirational speaker living in northern Wisconsin and Corpus Christi, Texas. She has two CD of original music, "Innocent Future" and "Solitaire." Her other books include "Party of Twelve: The Afterlife Interviews" and "Diaries of a Psychic Sorority," coauthored with Teresa McMillian and Lily Phelps. Together with Lily and Teresa, she researched and developed Conflict Revolution®, a revolutionary new way for dealing with conflict on a singular root level. They are currently conducting Conflict Revolution® workshops around the country.

For more information, visit www.barbarawith.com

Photo: Lois Carlson
Book layout and design: Barbara With